PYCNOGENOL:

The Super "Protector" Nutrient

Other Recent Books by Dr. Passwater

PYCNOGENOL:
The Super "Protector" Nutrient

**Richard A. Passwater, Ph.D.
and Chithan Kandaswami, Ph.D.**

Keats Publishing, Inc.   New Canaan, Connecticut

PYCNOGENOL: THE SUPER "PROTECTOR" NUTRIENT

Pycnogenol® is a registered trademark of Horphag Research, Limited, St. Peter Port, Guernsey, Channel Islands, U.K. Protected by U.S. Patent #4,698,360 and international patents.

Library of Congress Cataloging-in-Publication Data

Passwater, Richard A.
  Pycnogenol : the super "protector" nutrient / by Richard A. Passwater and Chithan Kandaswami.
    p. cm.
  Includes bibliographical references.
  ISBN: 0-87983-648-2 : $4.95
  1. Bioflavonoids—Physiological effect. 2. Antioxidants. I. Kandaswami, Chithan. II. Title.
QP772.B5P37   1994
613.2'8—dc20   94-20338
                                                     CIP

Printed in the United States of America

Published by Keats Publishing, Inc.
27 Pine Street, Box 876
New Canaan, Connecticut 06840-0876

CONTENTS

PYCNOGENOL:

The Super "Protector" Nutrient

1

The Benefits of Pycnogenol

NUTRITIONISTS are excited as research reveals an expanded understanding of the versatility of the complex of nutrients in Pycnogenol®. The ''super protector nutrient'' is actually more than a single nutrient. Pycnogenol (pronounced pick-nah-geh-nol) is a complex of powerful antioxidant nutrients that are patented for use to scavenge free radicals. The derivation of the name ''Pycnogenol'' has to do with the fact that many complex compounds are formed from simple units. Translated, this means that this specific mixture of nutrients can help you live better longer, stay healthier and appear more youthful. Pycnogenol can help protect you from approximately *eighty* diseases, including: heart disease, cancer, arthritis, and most other non-germ diseases that are linked to the deleterious chemical action of free radicals.

During the past 40 years, the pace of scientific study of the aging process has accelerated and now the free-radical theory of aging is well-supported with numerous studies. During the past five years, these confirming studies have become well known not just to the biochemists, such as your authors, doing the basic research, but even to practicing nutritionists and physicians. It is now well-established that antioxidant nutrients protect the body's cells from attack by very reactive chemicals called free radicals. These free radicals form during normal metabolism and are multiplied by environmental pollutants and radiation.

As scientists study the ways in which antioxidant nutrients protect the body from these harmful reactions that speed the aging process, cause cancer, heart disease and many other diseases, we strive to find better and better antioxidants. Nature has supplied us with the best antioxidants, and to our delight, we find that some of the most effective antioxidants are in Pycnogenol. The antioxidants of Pycnogenol, along with other antioxidant nutrients, provide outstanding protection. Besides being a powerful antioxidant in its own right, Pycnogenol also protects the antioxidant vitamin C.

In addition to its antioxidant protection that slows the damage associated with aging, Pycnogenol restores elasticity and smoothness to skin via its influence on skin protein formation. What is even more exciting, is that Pycnogenol is more than a powerful antioxidant. It nourishes blood cells, blood vessels and the skin. Pycnogenol is unique because it also alleviates hay fever and other allergies, and strengthens capillaries to reduce edema, bruising, and varicose veins. Together, these actions of Pycnogenol make it one of the most important nutrients.

Still, this information will be new to many, including health professionals. We mentioned that the pace of antioxidant research is quickening, but it hasn't been an easy accomplishment. In the 1970s, whenever one of your authors described the health benefits of antioxidants, medical professionals would scoff at the idea that so many conditions could be alleviated or prevented with antioxidants. The health professionals did not understand how free radicals attacked the body to cause or be involved with nearly eighty diseases. Nor did they understand how antioxidant nutrients protected against free-radical damage. Without this knowledge, it was impossible for them to understand how antioxidants protected us from so many different diseases. Thus, the typical reaction was disbelief and ridicule.

Fortunately, through the years many research reports appeared in medical as well as scientific journals. Now cardiologists, oncologists and many other medical specialists and health professionals understand how one group of nutrients can protect us against so many different—and seemingly unrelated—diseases. Just as fortunately, the general public was educated right along with the health profession as almost weekly reports in major newspapers and magazines kept abreast of the exciting research.

Why did medical and science writers report on these studies? Because antioxidant nutrients could save many, many people from the ravages of cancer and premature heart disease. In 1993, the Pracon Study found that antioxidant nutrients could save the U.S. public about nine *billion* dollars every year by reducing illness from the five leading causes of death, including cancer and heart disease.

This book will bring more exciting research on a powerful antioxidant to the public, as well as show other important benefits of Pycnogenol. European physicians have known since 1950 that Pycnogenol strengthened capillaries and reduced swelling in the legs and ankles. They have used Pycnogenol with great success against hay fever and allergies since 1960. In the 1970s, enthusiastic users called Pycnogenol "the skin vitamin" and the "skin cosmetic in a pill." However, it wasn't until 1986 that the great antioxidant power of Pycnogenol was fully realized.

This book will explain how this amazing nutrient protects us against so many diseases and helps overcome troublesome disorders such as allergies, inflammation, edema (water retention) and bruising. Table 1.1 lists the various health benefits of Pycnogenol that will be examined in this book.

Table 1.1
Health Benefits of Pycnogenol

Reduces risk of:
  Heart disease
  Cancer
  Accelerated aging
  Arthritis
  Oxidative stress and
  More than 70 other radical-related diseases

Table 1.1 continued

Strengthens blood vessels and . . .
  Maintains proper capillary permeability
  Reduces capillary fragility
  Reduces bruising
  Strengthens capillaries, veins and arteries
  Reduces the severity of sports injuries
  Reduces varicose veins
  Reduces edema and swelling of the legs
  Treats chronic venous insufficiency
  Reduces the risk of phlebitis
Red blood cells
  Improves red-blood-cell membrane flexibility
Skin health
  Improves skin elasticity
  Improves skin smoothness
  Effective against psoriasis
  Protects against sun damage
Allergies
  Very effective against hay fever
Inflammation
  Fights inflammation
  Improves joint flexibility
  Reduces the pain due to swollen joints
Diabetes
  Reduces diabetic retinopathy
Immune system
  Enhances immune response
  Reduces frequency and severity of colds
Ophthalmology
  Reduces retinopathies
  Help prevent capillary bleeding, floaters
Gastrointestinal
  Acts against stomach ulcers and inflammation

2

Pycnogenol: A Nutrient or an Herb?

PYCNOGENOL is a multi-talented nutrient performing many important functions and roles, but its roles are all nutritional. North American Indians used a tree-bark extract as an herbal medicine, but they were actually curing scurvy with vitamin C and flavonoids. Flavonoids are nutrients produced in many plants. When flavonoids are used by the body, they are often referred to as *bioflavonoids*. Most nutritionists prefer to use this generic term based on *function*, rather than specific flavonoid classes based merely on *structure*. In this book, we will generally use the term "bioflavonoid" to indicate nutritional function. In the "For the Health Professional" section of Chapter Three, we will discuss the flavonoid class *biflavonoid*. Bioflavonoid and biflavonoid are *different terms* and not mispellings.

The U.S. Food and Drug Administration (FDA) essentially defines nutrients and drugs as compounds that are one or the other. They consider that a nutrient only provides nourishment and does not aid any health disorder except a deficiency disease caused by a lack of that nutrient. A compound that claims to have any other effect on the body other than simple nourishment is considered a drug and must pass rigorous and expensive testing to demonstrate those effects.

However, many of us have provided evidence that nutrients alleviate or prevent many diseases in addition to the known deficiency diseases. In 1992, a major conference was sponsored by the New York Academy of Sciences entitled "Beyond Deficiency: New Views on the Function and Health Effects of Vitamins." For the first time, the vast body of "establishment" nutritionists and medical researchers witnessed a large body of very convincing evidence from academic biochemists that nutrients do indeed affect the health in areas beyond deficiency diseases. The media, including the *New York Times, TIME* magazine, and *Newsweek* picked up on the quiet revolution. The cover of *TIME* called attention to the fact that antioxidant nutrients prevented heart disease and cancer and slowed the aging process.

Nature doesn't go by our rules and definitions. The great efficiency and economy of Nature lets compounds perform many tasks. But, according to FDA regulations, even a vitamin is ruled a drug if it helps cure a disease other than a frank deficiency disease, or is advertised as affecting other body conditions or diseases. For instance, according to FDA regulations, if vitamin C prevents scurvy at 60 milligrams a day, it is indeed a vitamin. But, if the vitamin C is used to help control an allergy or to ward off a cold, then it is considered a drug and cannot be sold until it passes millions of dollars worth of tests and studies.

Herbs that have been in use as part of folklore before the FDA regulations went into effect are exempt from this regulation, unless a manufacturer advertises them for curing or alleviating diseases. In this book, we will follow the teachings of Nature and not worry about artificial definitions. However, you most likely want to know just what Pycnogenol is. Is Pycnogenol a nutrient, or an herb, or a drug? In this chapter, we will establish that Pycnogenol is a nutrient, even though it has historical use and application as an herb. As mentioned earlier, a pine-bark extract that seemed to be very similar to Pycnogenol was indeed used as an herb by North American Indians as far back at least as the 1500s to treat what is now known as scurvy. The "herbal" usage was really a nutritional use to potentiate the action of the sparse amount of vitamin C that was available in harsh Canadian winters.

Pycnogenol Restores Missing Nutrients

The definition of a nutrient is "a dietary substance that provides nourishment to the body." *The World Book Dictionary* defines nutrient as "a nourishing substance, especially as an element or ingredient of a foodstuff."[1] The same dictionary defines an herb as "a plant whose leaves or stems are used for medicine, seasoning, food or perfume." Add roots to that definition and it is good enough.

Bioflavonoids are significant dietary components. They are so important, they were once given vitamin status. Perhaps, after more study, the vitamin status will be restored to bioflavonoids. Until that time, we can best classify bioflavonoids as a "vitamin C helper." Both bioflavonoids and vitamin C are antioxidants, but each has roles independent of the other as well. However, since bioflavonoids spare vitamin C, any action of vitamin C can also be indirectly attributed to bioflavonoids. Vitamin C is needed to produce the skin protein, collagen. But, if vitamin C is destroyed before it can be used to produce collagen, then it is of little use. Now if Pycnogenol is available in the body to protect vitamin C, then vitamin C can do its job. Pycnogenol extends the amount of vitamin C available. If the production of collagen is limited because of an inadequate amount of vitamin C, adding Pycnogenol to the diet protects the vitamin C from destruction and thus the Pycnogenol helps collagen production, even though the collagen production is not a direct role of Pycnogenol.

Bioflavonoids are needed for the optimal health of capillaries and proper membrane elasticity of red blood cells. These are the major nutritional roles for bioflavonoids. Bioflavonoids are also part of Nature's arsenal of antioxidant nutrients that protect us against the oxidative stress that can lead to heart disease, cancer and dozens of other diseases. Nature provides us with these protective bioflavonoid nutrients in fruits and vegetables. There is no question that bioflavonoids are nutrients as they are in ample amounts in whole foods, and they have normal functions in the body. The only question is whether bioflavonoids should again be given vitamin status.

The quantity and variety of bioflavonoids have diminished in modern diets as people are eating fewer fruits and vegetables, and food processors throw bioflavonoids away because of their bitter taste. Only nine percent of Americans eat the recommended five daily servings of fruits and vegetables. That's less than one in ten people! Those fruits and vegetables that *are* consumed tend to be fractionated and processed so as to leave out the portions rich in bioflavonoids. Modern agricultural practices such as not allowing foods to fully ripen on the vine also tend to diminish the amounts and types of flavonoids present in our food. When you eat a naturally ripened "whole" fruit, you will likely eat a respectable amount of its bioflavonoids. But food processors find that they can process the food better if they remove a lot of the fiber, rind and skin. And again, since most bioflavonoids taste bitter, food processors produce a sweeter tasting preparation by throwing out the parts containing bioflavonoids. Thus, dietary choices, food processing and agricultural practices are combining to lessen the total quantity, quality and variety of bioflavonoids in modern diets.

Pycnogenol: Not an Herb or Drug

We really don't have to worry about semantics when considering the actions of Pycnogenol regarding whether it is a nutrient or a drug. Even when Pycnogenol is correcting bodily disorders, it is achieving the correction through nourishing the body.

Pycnogenol is a nutrient that corrects conditions because it strengthens capillaries, nourishes the skin, balances histamine production, etc. By restoring optimal health to body components such as capillaries, Pycnogenol can correct disorders such as edema and microbleeding. Pycnogenol does not create an artificial compensatory mechanism to correct, but restores normal function and condition.

Just because the first historical use of Pycnogenol seemed to be herbal (there is always necessity and interest in curing problems rather than in preventing them), does not take away from the fact that Pycnogenol is a nutrient that helps maintain normal body function.

The FDA and the Public's Interest

Now the FDA does have a reason for making the definitions to distinguish between nutrients and drugs. They are rightfully concerned that nutrients might be sold with unproven drug claims. They are also concerned with the public safety and they wish to make sure that quantities used are indeed safe. *Primum non nocere*—first do no harm. Even though most nutrients are not subjected to extensive toxicity tests because of the expense of such tests, Pycnogenol has been extensively tested with proper toxicity studies over decades. The studies include acute and gross toxicity, mutagenicity, carcinogenic and teratogenic studies (birth defects). Pycnogenol passed with flying colors, it is extremely safe, in the same class as vitamin C.

Pycnogenol would not have been allowed to be sold in so many countries for so many years, if it were not a safe nutrient. As long as Pycnogenol continues to be sold without drug-like claims, it is in the public's interest to have Pycnogenol available as a nutrient-rich food supplement.

REFERENCE

1. Barnhart, Clarence L. and Barnhart, Robert K., *The World Book Dictionary.* Doubleday & Co., New York (1978).

3

Flavonoids and Similar Nutrients

FOR far too long a time, nutritionists concentrated on the macronutrients—carbohydrates, fats, proteins—and almost ignored the micronutrients. During the 1980s, vitamins and minerals began receiving the attention they deserve, but it has been only recently that flavonoids and carotenoids have received any appreciable attention. There is a great deal of similarity between these two chemically distinct classes of nutrients. The similarities will give these nutrients great respect as the 1990s lead us into the next century.

The great importance of flavonoids and carotenoids lies in their antioxidant and anti-free radical properties. Bioflavonoids and carotenoids are found in fruits and vegetables, which are unfortunately scarce in the typical American diet. You don't have to understand the biochemistry of these nutrients, or their differences in chemical structures, to appreciate how Pycnogenol protects you. However, you may be interested in knowing a little about how flavonoids fit into the overall picture.

Both flavonoids and carotenoids provide most of the beautiful colors of our fruits and vegetables. Chlorophyll provides the green, but most of the yellows, oranges and reds are carotenoids. The blues, purples, emerald green and some reds are flavonoids. Perhaps we should start with carotenoids as many people are familiar with the carotenoid beta-carotene.

Hundreds of carotenoids are commonly found in fruits and vegetables. Carotenoids are antioxidants, antiradicals and singlet oxygen quenchers, plus it appears that they may participate in improving gap junction communication. There is strong evidence including mechanistic studies, animal studies, epidemiological and clinical intervention studies indicating that carotenoids reduce the risk of cancer, and there is appreciable (but not yet conclusive) evidence that they protect against heart disease.

There are two families of carotenoids, the carotenes, which contain only carbon and hydrogen atoms, and the xanthophylls, which also contain oxygen atoms. Common carotenes include the alpha- and beta-carotenes so abundant in carrots, and lycopene, which gives the characteristic red coloring to tomatoes. Some carotenes are converted into vitamin A in the body. An example of a common xanthophyll is the capsanthin of red paprika. Carotenoids have chemical structures vastly different from flavonoids. Carotenoids have 40 carbon atoms including "conjugated" double bonds flanked by 6-carbon member rings or near rings at each end, plus 10 single side chains or substitutions.

Although over 600 different *carotenoids* have been characterized, they are simply divided into two families. There are more than 4,000 chemically unique *flavonoids* (or phenylchromes) that have been identified in plants. This is only a small fraction of the total number that are likely to be present in Nature, since only a few plants have been systematically examined for their flavonoid constituents. Unlike the alkaloids which are restricted to about 20 percent of the flowering plant species, flavonoids occur universally in vascular plants.

The chemical structures of flavonoids are based on 15 carbon atoms that include a Chromane Ring bearing a second aromatic ring on the second, third or fourth carbon atom. (See Figure 3.1.) Although flavonoids have the same basic structure, they still have a striking structural diversity. It is doubtful whether any other class of natural compounds exhibit the myriad of pharmacological effects which the flavonoids display. It is important to remember that they are grouped together because they have a similar chemical *structure*. They are *not* necessarily grouped together because of *biochemical* similarities—which do vary—but are grouped solely by their structural similarities.

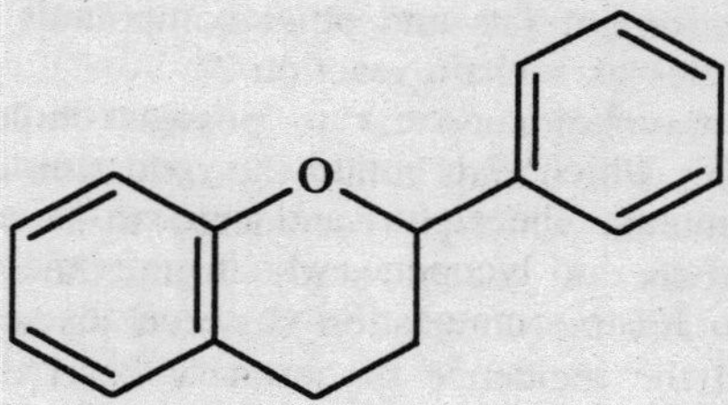

Figure 3.1: Basic structure of flavonoids

In humans, flavonoids participate in phospholipid metabolism, arachidonic acid metabolism, protein phosphorylation, calcium ion translocation, free-radical scavenging, redox reactions, antioxidant activity, chelation and gene expression. Flavonoids are known to display a bewildering array of biochemical actions. They have long been recognized to display beneficial actions against the following:

- inflammation
- allergy
- microorganisms (infection)
- parasites (worms, helminths)
- liver diseases
- vascular diseases
- thrombosis (clotting)
- viruses
- cancer
- toxic chemicals (including cancer-causing chemicals)
- coronary artery disease (atherosclerosis and myocardial infarction)

The health-promoting effects of several flavonoids continue to be recognized in many experimental situations. Some influence the activity of cells that affect the immune system. This has profound implications for cancer prevention. Flavonoids are powerful antioxidants. They act as free-radical scavengers and block the undesirable degradation (oxidation) of fats and other compounds which proceed in cycles as a chain reaction.

Certain flavonoids appear to possess cholesterol-lowering effects. Flavonoids retard the oxidation of low-density lipoproteins which is considered to be involved in atherosclerosis. A recent study from the Netherlands showed an inverse correlation between dietary flavonoid intake and the incidence of coronary heart disease. The individuals with the lowest dietary intake of flavonoids had the highest incidence of heart disease. Interestingly, the relative incidence of heart disease among men who had the highest intake of flavonoids was only a third of those who had the lowest intake of flavonoids. The results were the same after adjustment for age, body fat, smoking, cholesterol, blood pressure, physical activity, coffee consumption and the intake of calories, vitamin C, vitamin E, beta-carotene and dietary fiber.

An interesting relationship has been shown to exist between flavonoids and vitamin C. Flavonoids have been reported to protect vitamin C and preserve its action. They have been shown to increase absorption of vitamin C in human volunteers.[12]

Some flavonoids, such as those in Pycnogenol, are especially potent antioxidants, metal chelators and free-radical scavengers. They are powerful radical-chain-breaking antioxidants. They can sequester and thus reduce the activity of the deleterious oxidant-inducing metals such as ''free'' iron and copper ions. The flavonoids of Pycnogenol possess vitamin C-sparing activities and promote collagen production. They improve capillary resistance and permeability and decrease the fragility of the capillary walls.

They also are protective against UV-B solar radiation and can inhibit histamine release from neutrophils, mast cells, eosinophils, etc. of the reticuloendothelial system. This antihistamine effect is of great interest from the standpoint of allergy control. The major advantages of Pycnogenol are its water-solubility (it is produced by water extraction) and its great bioavailability.

Like the carotenoids, flavonoids were once divided into two main classes. The two main classes of flavonoids were the anthocyanins and anthoxanthins. These classification systems differ in their criteria and thus, they even differ in the number of "families" they create. We recognize that some researchers will prefer different classification systems than the one we follow, but our main objective is to keep biochemistry as uncomplicated as possible for readers who choose not to be burdened with biochemical jargon.

Even scientists often confuse the terms "flavonoid" and "bioflavonoid." The flavonoids are members of a family of compounds called *polyphenols*, which merely means that they have more than one phenol group. Bioflavonoids are, of course, included in that description, but they are further defined as having biochemical utility. Some formal classification systems include a separate family called "bioflavonoids," while others do not. In this book we will simply use the term bioflavonoid to depict biochemically active flavonoids.

Flavonoids are found in fruits, vegetables, nuts, seeds, grains, and in beverages such as tea, cocoa and wine. Flavonoids are prominent components of citrus fruits and soybeans. The nutrition-minded have long known of bioflavonoids such as quercetin, rutin and hesperidin. However, recent scientific studies reported in the press have made the public aware of the flavonoids found in red wine, green tea, *Ginkgo biloba*, *Silybum marianum* and bilberry. Flavonoids generally occur bound to plant sugars as glycosides. During intestinal absorption, the free flavonoid is split off and released from the sugar.

Flavonoids are usually thought of as being "minor"

dietary constituents. They are minor in terms of the great quantity of carbohydrate, fat and protein consumed, but they are far from being trace nutrients. The magnitude of flavonoids in the diet is larger than many realize. Today, normal diets may contain 200 milligrams or so, and vegetarian diets may provide more than a gram (1,000 milligrams). However, as discussed earlier, this pales in comparison to the amounts formerly eaten before extensive food processing and poor dietary habits.

Bioflavonoids were once given greater importance to our health than what they receive today. Dr. Albert Szent-Gyorgyi was awarded the Nobel Prize in Medicine in 1937 for isolating what he at first in 1928 called "hexuronic acid." This is now called ascorbic acid or vitamin C. Dr. Szent-Gyorgyi noted that crude extracts from lemon juice were more effective against scurvy in guinea pigs than the pure ascorbic acid. Drs. Szent-Gyorgyi and S. Rusznyak found that in pathological conditions characterized by increased permeability or fragility of the capillaries, vitamin C was ineffective, whereas the condition could readily be cured by the administration of crude lemon juice or extracts of Hungarian red pepper.

In 1936, Drs. Szent-Gyorgyi and Rusznyak isolated a complex from lemon rind which they called "citrin." Citrin was further fractionated and the active ingredient was found to be in the fraction consisting of practically pure flavone or flavonol glucoside (eriodictoyl and hesperidin). They named this fraction of the extract "vitamin P" because it normalized the low capillary resistance of vascular purpura patients and also normalized vascular wall permeability. Continued experiments showed that citrin had the property of preventing the breakdown of capillaries in the body, prolonging the lives of guinea pigs affected by scurvy, and reducing the signs of vitamin C deficiency in experimental animals. These were the first reports of the therapeutic effects of plant flavonoids.

Dr. Szent-Gyorgyi requested others to duplicate his experiments. The results were mixed. The reason, Drs. Szent-

Gyorgyi and Bentsath discovered later, is that "Vitamin P requires for its activity the presence of traces of vitamin C." In 1971, Dr. Szent-Gyorgyi remarked in an introduction to a book on the anti-inflammatory action of flavonoids by Dr. Miklos Gabor:

"American science did not take in a friendly spirit to vitamin P and the name 'vitamin' was dropped. More than that, discussions have been going on to strike the flavones altogether from the list of [nutrients and] drugs, since no therapeutic action has been found. I think the contradiction is due to the fact that in the USA citrus fruits belong to people's regular daily diet [in those days]. They are rich in flavones, so a [total] lack in flavones is very rare, and if there is no deficiency, a vitamin has no action. In contrast to this, in countries where citrus fruits are expensive, the lack of flavones may cause trouble and their medication may show favorable effects. While these discussions were going on, important experimental material was collected in Hungary which, in my mind, *leaves no doubt about the vitamin nature and the biological activity of flavones.*" (Italics are the authors'.)

In our opinion, the contradictory results probably arose from a combination of two factors: 1) the difficulty of obtaining a completely flavonoid-free diet and 2) the failure to use vitamin C-free preparations of natural flavonoids. It is also likely that if Dr. Szent-Gyorgyi worked with the highly water-soluble flavonoids of Pycnogenol, the results may have been more striking and consistent.

A major difficulty in assessing flavonoid potency is that there is no simple test for the assessment of potency or for detection of possible deficiency. In the case of human studies, it is impossible to use control groups in view of the ubiquitous presence of flavonoids in most foodstuffs. Typical diets do not have optimal amounts of flavonoids, but they have enough to prevent total deficiency.

The situation is further complicated by the apparent interrelationships between flavonoids and specific nutrients, and in particular, vitamin C. At this juncture, it is worth mentioning that it is not known whether the health benefits attributed to vitamin C-containing fruits and vegetables are due to vitamin C per se, or due to the combined and concerted actions of vitamin C and bioflavonoids.

Flavonoids have been considered semi-essential nutrients years after they were dropped from the vitamin spectrum. In a certain sense, they have been designated as growth factors which permit optimal growth and well-being. Their multiple health-promoting activities have been increasingly appreciated in a myriad of experimental systems. Today, scientists such as Hungary's Dr. Miklos Gabor, have produced what they believe is "avitaminosis P," a vitamin P deficiency disease by using flavonoid-free diets. The future may well show the bioflavonoids to be true vitamins after all. Future work may throw light as to their vitamin function.

Comparison to Vitamin E

The tocopherols (vitamin E) are *monophenolic* compounds, that is, they contain only one phenol group. Alpha-tocopherol, beta-tocopherol, gamma-tocopherol and delta-tocopherol all have vitamin E activity to varying degrees. The tocopherols and flavonoids share a common chemical structure, the Chromane Ring shown in Figure 3.2. The chemical structure of alpha-tocopherol is depicted in Figure 3.3.

The more advanced and greater structural complexity of flavonoids and their greater number of phenolic groups give them greater biochemical versatility than the monophenolic vitamin E. It is not surprising that some of the bioflavonoids of Pycnogenol have many of the antioxidant properties of vitamin E and even exceed vitamin E in some antioxidant activities. Pycnogenol can be thought of as a very water-soluble super vitamin E in terms of its antioxidant power, but of course, Pycnogenol can't replace

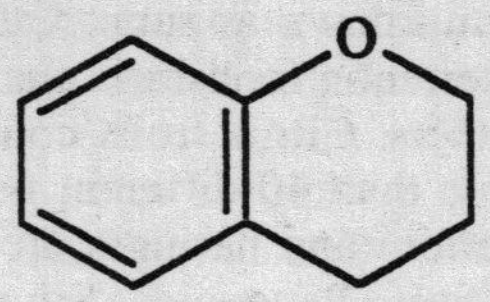

Figure 3.2: The Chromane Ring structure

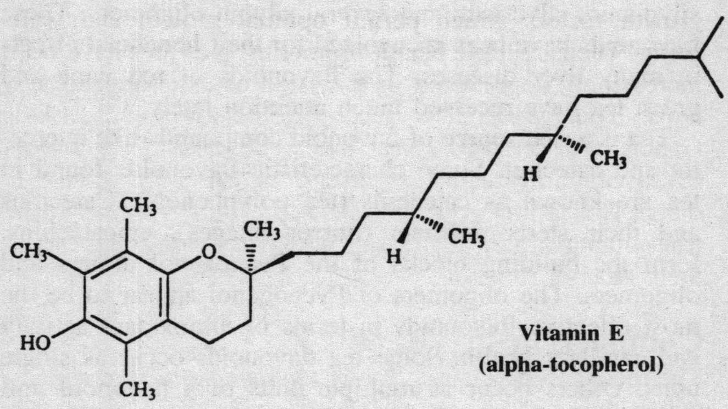

**Vitamin E
(alpha-tocopherol)**

Figure 3.3: Structure of Alpha-tocopherol (Chromane Ring)

fat-soluble vitamin E, which is essential to the diet and needed for internal membrane and lipoprotein protection. We need vitamin E, bioflavonoids, carotenoids, and other antioxidants for optimal health.

Other Flavonoid Classes

We don't intend to go into great detail about the chemical structures of the various flavonoids in this section, but we wish to show a couple to illustrate the subtle structural differences between flavonoid families. Quercetin, one of the most common and abundant flavonoids, occurs bound to sugars in a form known as rutin. Quercetin is found in high amounts in common foodstuffs such as apples, onions and tea, among others. Citrus fruits contain a wide variety of flavonoids. More than 40 different flavonoids are found in oranges. Hesperidin and naringin are some of the commonly occurring citrus flavonoids. Silymarin is a pharmacologically active flavonoid complex extracted from the seeds of the milk thistle, *Silybum marianum*. Silymarin contains a group of flavonoids called *flavanolignans* which include the flavonoids silybin, isosilybin, dehydrosilybin, silydianin, silycristin and several silybin oligomers. These flavonoids have been recognized for their beneficial effects in many liver diseases. The flavonoids of red wine and green tea have received much attention lately.

Tea is a rich source of flavonoid compounds like quercetin and catechin. Some characteristic flavonoids found in tea are known as catechins (tea polyphenols). Catechins and their stereo isomers (mirror images), epicatechins, form the building blocks of the Pycnogenol dimers and oligomers. The oligomers of Pycnogenol appear to be the most effective flavonoids in terms of antioxidant activity and capillary health. Some tea flavonoids occur as single units. Others occur as multiple units of a flavonoid unit (condensed forms). These multiple forms are produced during fermentation of the tea. Green tea contains certain unique flavonoids (catechin derivatives).

A rich variety of flavonoids are also found in evergreen trees or shrubs. The flavonoid pigments known as anthocyanins are almost universally found in the flowering plants. They are responsible for the attractive scarlet to blue colors of flowers, fruits, leaves, fruit juices and wines. The pigmentation of red grapes and red wine is due to anthocyanin flavonoids. Different varieties of berries contain a host of flavonoid compounds. Bilberry is rich in anthocyanins and other flavonoids. Research has shown these flavonoids to help night vision. Soybeans are particularly rich in a class of flavonoids termed as isoflavonoids. One common example of this class is genistein which is present in soy products. Genistein has received a great deal of attention as a potential anticancer agent.

The Important Advantages of Pycnogenol

Pycnogenol is of special interest because it not only contains simple bioflavonoids such as catechins and epicatechins, it also contains dimers and oligomers of catechins and epicatechins, as well as organic acids. This combination is a well-controlled symphony of fast-acting bioflavonoids and long-lasting, potent oligomers. The most potent antiradicals are the dimeric proanthocyanidins. Epicatechins and catechins, as well as the organic acids of Pycnogenol such as caffeic acid, inhibit the formation of many reactive oxygen species less than the dimeric proanthocyanidins, however, they are clearly much more effective than vitamin C in this regard.

Plant flavonoids are generally not soluble in water. Pycnogenol, produced solely by warm-water extraction under pressure, is water-soluble. This means that Pycnogenol is well-absorbed and bioavailable. This is why it is so effective as a powerful antioxidant and capillary strengthener as you will see in the later chapters.

Note in Figures 3.4a and 3.4b that removing the double bond between carbons number two and three of the flavone structure makes a "flavanone," and in Figure 3.5, that adding a hydroxyl group at carbon number three of the flavone makes a "flavonol." The flavone, flavonol and flavonone families can be grouped together as part of a larger class (the anthoxanthin class of the "old" two-class system is one example). Many flavonols are yellow, while several flavones and flavonones are colorless.

Catechin has the chemical structure shown in Figure 3.6. Note that it has five hydroxyl (OH) groups, which make it a potent antioxidant. A very slight variation is called epicatechin which is illustrated in Figure 3.7. These bioflavonoids are important to us, as they—and their substituted family members—are the building blocks for the

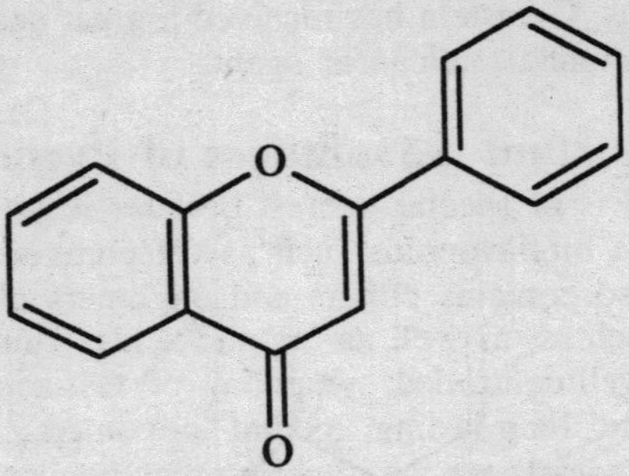

Figure 3.4a: Basic structure of flavones

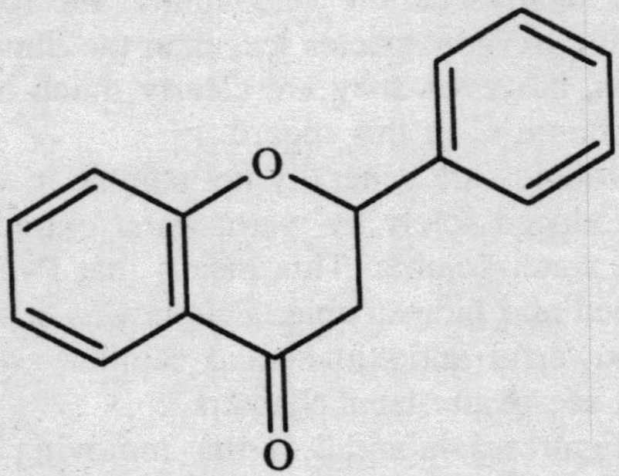

Figure 3.4b: Basic structure of flavanones

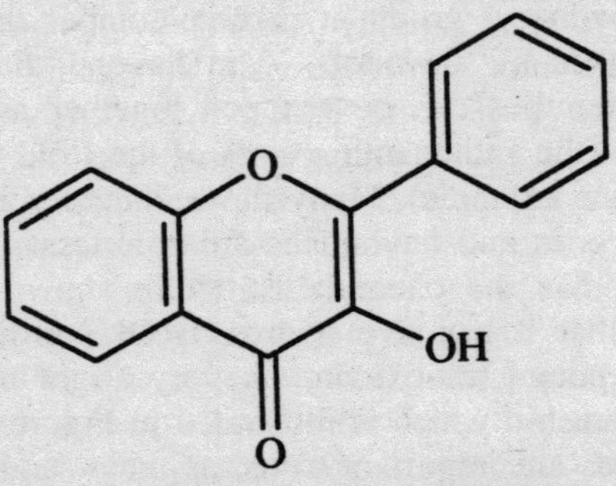

Figure 3.5: Basic structure of flavonols

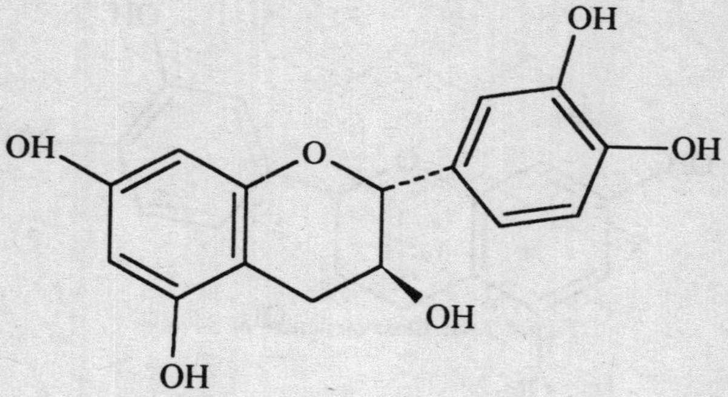

Figure 3.6: (+)-Catechin

proanthocyanidin dimers, trimers and oligomers that constitute the major bioflavonoids of Pycnogenol. Figures 3.8a, b and c shows some typical dimers of Pycnogenol and Figure 3.9 illustrates an oligomer of Pycnogenol.

Proanthocyanidins (PACs) are a family of flavonoids so named because they can be hydrolyzed to produce the pigment that gives the reddish color to red cabbage. The PACs are made formed from chains of catechins which combine with epinegatively charged epicatechins in a multitude of different combinations. Pycnogenol is approximately 80 to 85 percent PACs, 5 percent catechin and epicatechin and 2 to 4 percent organic acids such as caffeic acid that are the precursors of catechin and epicatechin. We'll take a more detailed look into the composition of Pycnogenol in the next chapter.

How did this complex and powerful blend of bioflavonoids originate? That is an interesting tale going back before the sixteenth century. We'll take a look at the historical significance of Pycnogenol in Chapter Five. If you are a health professional, you will be interested in the

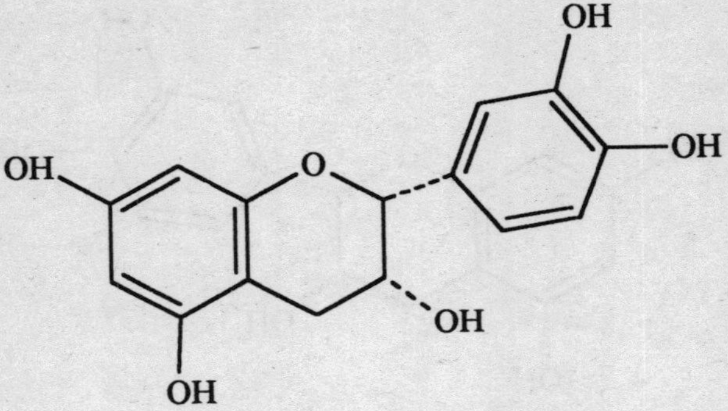

Figure 3.7: (-)-Epicatechin

technical discussions that follow. Otherwise, the general reader may wish to skip over this technical section and move directly to Chapter Four.

For the Health Professional

Polyphenolic compounds are found in all flowering plants (phanerogamic species).[1] Included within this group of compounds are phenolic acids, flavonoids, lignins, etc. [1-3, 15-17] These aromatic compounds are formed in plants from the aromatic amino acid phenylalanine and acetate units. The flavonoids constitute the majority of plant polyphenols. Caffeic acids (e.g. curcumin from turmeric) have partial flavonoid structures (cinnamyol fragments).

On average, our daily diet may contain 200 milligrams to one gram of mixed flavonoids. The dietary intake of flavonoids far exceeds that of vitamin E, a monophenolic antioxidant, and beta-carotene.[19,20] Resurgence of interest in traditional medicine during the past two decades, to-

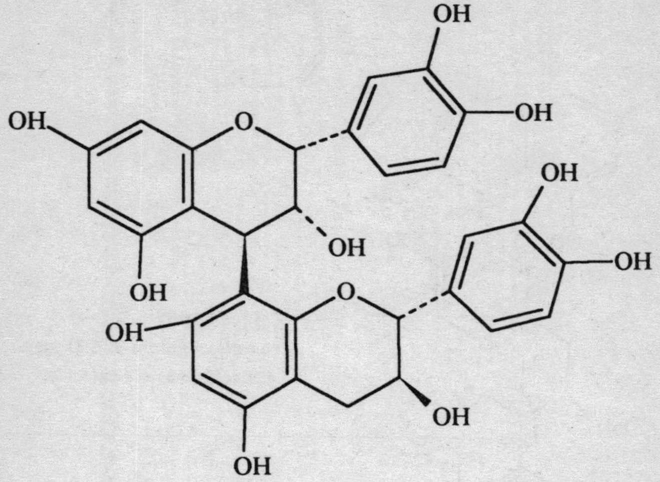

Figure 3.8a: Proanthocyanidin B-1 Dimer
Epicatechin-(4b-8')-catechin

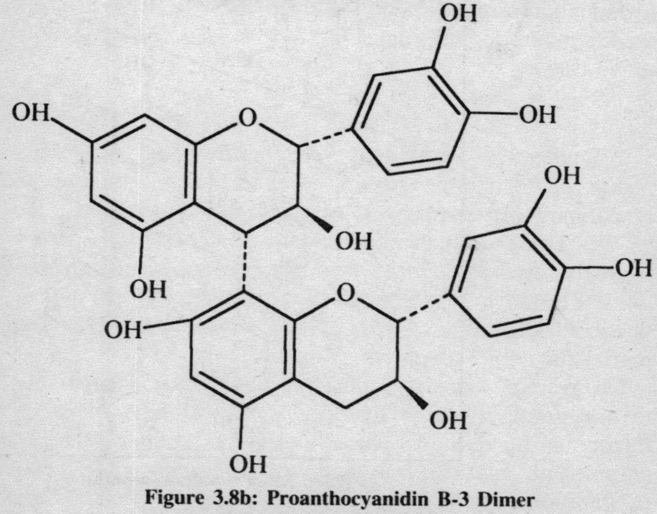

Figure 3.8b: Proanthocyanidin B-3 Dimer
Catechin-4a-8')-catechin

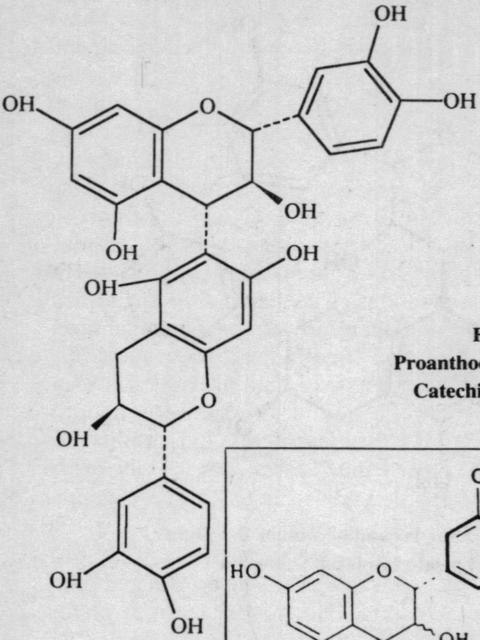

Figure 3.8c:
Proanthocyanidin B-6 Dimer
Catechin-(4a-6')-catechin

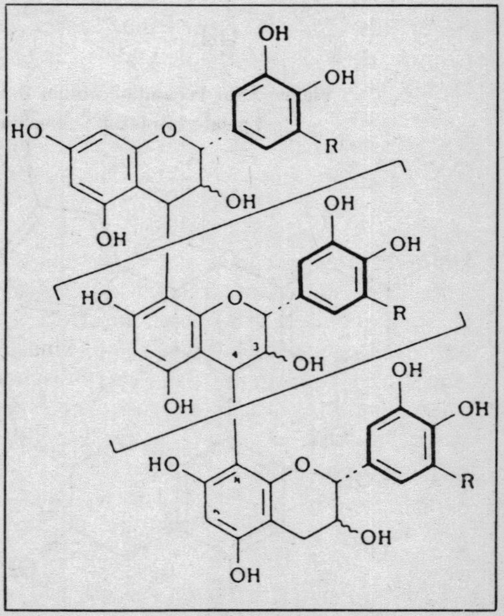

Figure 3.9: Proanthocyanindin
(n=0,1,2,3,4,5-----)

gether with an expanded effort in pharmacognosy, have
rekindled interest in the flavonoids and the need to understand their interactions with mammalian cells and tissues.
Flavonoids are known to display a bewildering array of
nutritional, pharmacological and biochemical actions. They
have long been recognized to possess anti-inflammatory,
antiallergic, antiviral, anticarcinogenic, antineoplastic, anti-
microbial, antihelminthic, liver protective, antithrombotic
and antihormonal activities. Their potential health-promoting activities have come to be increasingly appreciated in
many experimental situations. The flavonoids are typical
phenolic compounds and therefore act as potent antioxidants, metal chelators and free-radical scavengers.[9,21-22]
They are powerful chain-breaking antioxidants. They inhibit the oxidative modification of low-density lipoproteins.[23] The potential advantages of the ability of
flavonoids to sequester and thus reduce the activity of the
dangerous oxidant-inducing metals such as iron and copper
cannot be overemphasized.

Flavonoids function as light screens in plants. They protect the plant DNA from ultraviolet radiation-induced damage. Flavonoids and vitamin C occur together in plants.
They appear to be mutually protective. Interestingly, flavonoids are known to possess vitamin C stabilizing and
antioxidant-dependent vitamin C-sparing activities.[13,14,24]
They are also known to increase the absorption of vitamin
C.[12,14] Flavonoids are known to affect a large number of
enzyme systems including protein kinase C, protein tyrosine kinases, phospholipase A-2, phospholipase C, reverse
transcriptase, ornithine decarboxylase, sialidase, nucleotide
phosphodiesterases, lipoxygenases, cytochrome P450-de-
pendent oxygenases, glutathione-S-transferase, and
aromatase, among others.[7] Some of these enzyme systems
appear to be critically involved in chronic diseases and
several disease states including cancer.

Studies with mammalial cell systems indicate that certain flavonoids, depending on structure, can alter the function of mast cells, basophils, neutrophils, eosinophils,

monocytes/macrophages, B and T lymphocytes, platelets, nerve, smooth muscle and various cancer cells.[7,8] The physiological and pathological processes affected by flavonoids include secretion, neurotransmitter release mitogenesis, antigen presentation, lipid peroxidation, platelet aggregation and adhesion to endothelial surfaces, cell motility and malignant cell proliferation, and the function/expression of adhesion molecules.[7] No other class of chemicals seems to exhibit such diverse and numerous nutritional and biochemical actions in mammalian cells.

Definitions, Nomenclatures and Structures

The polyphenols are aromatic compounds with multiple hydroxyl (OH) groups. The simple phenols have only one ring (benzene) with hydroxyl groups attached to their ring structure. Phenols or polyphenols containing the cinnamoyl structure are designated as cinnamoyl derivatives. In plants, the aromatic amino acids, phenylalanine and tyrosine, are converted to cinnamic acids which condense with acetate units to form the core structure (cinnamoyl structure) of the flavonoids. This structure is also known as the cinnamoyl fragment. A vast array of phenolic acids such as curcumin (found in turmeric), caffeic acid, chlorogenic acid, etc., are cinnamic acid derivatives and are therefore, partial flavonoids. Biotransformation of flavonoids in the gut can release these cinnamic acid derivatives (phenolic acids).

The flavonoids are phenylchromones (1,4-benzopyrones or benzo-gamma-pyrones) possessing a 15-carbon structure. The common structure can also be described as a benzene ring (A) condensed with a g-pyrone ring (C) having a phenyl ring (B) substituted at position 2 or 3. A phenyl group is usually substituted at the 2-position of the pyrone ring. In isoflavonoids, the substitution is at the 3-position. The flavonoids are highly complex molecules. Based on their substitution patterns, one could envision the occurrence of hundreds of thousands of flavonoids. A few of the substituted flavonoids are found as derivatives with methoxy and sulfate groups. In foods, flavonoids are usually bound to sugars such as glucose, galactose, glucorhamnose, rhamnose, or arabinose. Sugar substitution (glycosylation) can occur at various hydroxyl groups of the molecule.[1-3] Flavonoids occasionally are found in plants having methyl or acetyl substitution.

The main structural classes of flavonoids can be listed as follows:

- flavans, flavanols and proanthocyanidins
- flavones and flavonols
- anthocyanins
- isoflavonoids
- flavanones
- flavanonoles
- biflavonoids (note: this is not bioflavonoids)
- chalcones and aurones
- neoflavones

Most of the flavonoids are lipid soluble (lipophilic or hydrophobic molecules) and are of relatively low molecular weight for bioactive components of foods. The complex Pycnogenol is a water-soluble form.

The flavonols possess a hydroxyl group at the 3-position of the flavone ring. Common examples are quercetin, kaempferol and myricetin. Rutin is a glycoside of quercetin. The flavones lack the above 3-hydroxyl group. Some examples are luteolin and apigenin. The isoflavones (e.g. genistein) have their phenyl group attached to the 3-position of the pyrone moiety. Flavones, flavonols and isoflavones possess a 2,3-double bond which is not there in flavanones, flavanonols, flavans (flavanols), anthocyanins and proanthocyanidins. Flavone lacking the 2,3-double bond becomes flavanonol (e.g. taxifolin). The 4-position of flavones, flavonols, isoflavonoids, flavonones and flavanonols possess an oxygen atom at the 4-position. There is no substitution at this position in anthocyanidins (e.g. pelargonidin, cyanidin).

The anthocyanins are glycosides of anthocyanidins. Anthocyanidins are water-soluble pigments. All the colorless substances isolated from plants which when heated with acid form anthocyanidins are collectively designated as proanthocyanidins. This is a chemical term and does not imply any biosynthetic relationship. The term leukoanthocyanidin was reserved for the monomeric (i.e. single structural unit) proanthocyanidins such as flavan-4-ols or flavan-3,4-diols. The name proanthocyanidin (or condensed proanthocyanidins) was used for flavan-3-ol dimers (two condensed units), higher oligomers (multiple bound structural units) and polymers. Compounds with an unsubstituted middle-ring (C-ring) are called flavans. Flavans with a hydroxyl substitution at the 3-position are called flavan-3-ols. A common example is catechin which is widespread in plants. Catechin belongs to the class of procyanidin within the proanthocyanidin group. This is the largest class of monomeric flavans. The monomers, flavan-3-ols and flavan-3,4-diols possess hydroxyl substitutions at the 3- and, both 3- and 4- positions, respectively. Like quercetin, catechin and its derivatives are widely distributed in the plant kingdom.

The basic units—catechin and its substituted family members—and its stereo isomer (mirror image) epicatechin— and its substituted family members—can combine together in many different ways and combinations. This can be illustrated by allowing "c" to stand for catechin, and "e' to represent epicatechin building blocks. These two basic units can combine in three ways—c-c (both components are catechins), e-e (both units are epicatechins) or c-e (one unit of each). The variations increase with each additional unit added—c-c-c, c-c-e, c-e-e, c-e-c, e-c-e, and e-e-e.

But Nature doesn't stop there. Nature allows these basic units to combine at different places in their structures.

Eight dimers have been identified in Pycnogenol and are simply called dimer B-1 through B-8.

You can imagine the combinations possible as the chain grows longer. Additionally, other flavonoids may also combine with the catechins' and epicatechins' basic units. Pycnogenol is indeed a complicated blend that is determined by consistency of starting material and extraction parameters.

The ratio of oxygen atoms to carbon atoms in the center heterocyclic ring is affected by the amount of double bonds and substitution. This oxygen to hydrogen ratio (sometimes called the oxidation index) is profoundly important in determining the spatial configuration and redox status which in turn determine the biochemical activity of the various flavonoids. The configuration of the flavan-3-ols of Pycnogenol provide superior biochemical properties. Most flavonoids appear biochemically inert and/or relatively insoluble and not very bioavailable by comparison.

Biflavonoids—note: *bi*flavonoids, not *bio*flavonoids—are two flavone structures bonded together. Remember, we use the term "bioflavonoid" to indicate flavonoids having biological activity. Now we are referring to the specific family of flavonoids that have the common structure of two flavones bonded together. Amentoflavone is an example of the class biflavonoid group. It is biapigenin. The term neoflavonoid refers to a group of naturally occurring compounds which are structurally and biosynthetically related to the flavonoids and to the isoflavonoids. Coumarin derivatives constitute one sub-class of neoflavonoids. The chalcones do not have the middle ring. They are intermediates in the biosynthesis of flavonoids in plants.

Tannins are polymers of flavanols. Their size is much larger than the sizes of oligomers and their antiradical activity is much less. However, tannins can be boiled with animal skin to treat skin fibers so as to produce leather. Tannins do retain some antiviral activity.

The tocopherols (vitamin E) are monophenolic compounds, that is, they contain only one phenol group.

Alpha-tocopherol, beta-tocopherol, gamma-tocopherol and delta-tocopherol all have vitamin E activity to varying degrees. The flavonoids are phenylchromones and phenylchromanes. The tocopherols and flavonoids share a common chemical structure, the chromane or chromone ring (Figure 3.2). The chemical structure of alpha-tocopherol is depicted in Figure 3.3.

As mentioned earlier, flavonoids can occur as thousands of distinctly different chemical structures, in view of the innumerable substitution patterns possible. The more advanced and greater structural complexity of flavonoids and their greater number of phenolic groups give them greater biochemical versatility than the monophenolic vitamin E and even exceed vitamin E in some antioxidant activities. Pycnogenol can be thought of as a very water-soluble super vitamin E in terms of its antioxidant power, but of course, Pycnogenol can't replace fat-soluble vitamin E which is essential to the diet and needed for internal membrane and lipoprotein protection. We need vitamin E, vitamin C, bioflavonoids, carotenoids, and other antioxidants for optimal health.

REFERENCES

1. Harborne, J. B., Mabry, T. J., Mabry, M. *The Flavonoids*. Academic Press, New York (1975).

2. Harborne, J. B., Mabry, T. J., *The Flavonoids: Advances in Research*. Chapman and Hall, London (1982).

3. Harborne, J. B., *The Flavonoids: Advances in Research Since 1980*. Chapman and Hall, London (1988).

4. Cody, V., Middleton, E. and Harborne, J. B., *Plant Flavonoids in Biology and Medicine: Biochemical, Pharmacological and Structure-Activity Relationships*. Alan R. Liss, Inc., New York (1986).

5. Cody, V., Middleton, E., Harborne, J. B. and Beretz, A., *Plant Flavonoids in Biology and Medicine II: Biochemical, Cellular, and Medicinal Properties*. Alan R. Liss, Inc., New York (1988).

6. Das, N. P., *Flavonoids in Biology and Medicine III.* National University of Singapore, Singapore (1989).

7. Middleton, E., Jr. and Kandaswami, C., *The Flavonoids: Advances in Research Since 1986* (J. B. Harborne, ed.). Chapman & Hall, London, 619 (1993).

8. Middleton, E., Jr. and Kandaswami, C., *Biochem. Pharmacol.* 43:1167 (1992).

9. Kandaswami, C. and Middleton, E., Jr., *Free Radicals in Diagnostic Medicine: A Systems Approach to Laboratory Technology, Clinical Correlations in Antioxidant Therapy* (D. Armstrong, ed.) Plenum Press, New York (in preparation).

10. Middleton, E., Jr. and Kandaswami, C., *Pharmacological Action of Flavonoids* (in preparation).

11. Hertog, M. G. L., et al., *Lancet* 342:1007 (1993).

12. Jones, E. and Hughes, R. E., *IRCS Med. Sci.* 12:320 (1984).

13. Clemetson, C. A. B., Anderson, L. *Ann, N.Y. Sci.* 136:341 (1966).

14. Hughes, R. E. and Wilson, H. K., *Progress in Medicinal Chemistry* (G. P. Ellis and G. B. West eds.). Elsevier, Amsterdam. 14:285–301 (1977).

15. Harborne, J. B., *Plant Flavonoids in Biology and Medicine: Biochemical, Pharmacological and Structure-Activity Relationships* (V. Cody, E. Middleton and J. B. Harborne, eds.). Alan R. Liss, New York, 15 (1986).

16. Harborne, J. B., *Plant Flavonoids in Biology and Medicine: Biochemical, Cellular, and Medicinal Properties* (V. Cody, E. Middleton and J. B. Harborne, eds.), Alan R. Liss, New York, 17 (1988).

17. Ebel, J. and Hahlbrock, K., *The Flavonoids: Advances in Research* (J. B. Harborne and T. J. Mabry, eds.). Chapman and Hall, London, p. 641 (1982).

18. Brouillard, R., and Cheminant, A., *Plant Flavonoids in Biology and Medicine: Biochemical, Cellular and Medicinal Properties* (V. Cody, E. Middleton and J. B. Harborne eds.). Alan R. Liss, New York, 93 (1988).

19. Pierpoint, W. S., *Plant Flavonoids in Biology and Medicine: Biochemical, Pharmacological and Structure-Activity Relationships* (V. Cody, E. Middleton and J. B. Harborne, eds.). Alan R. Liss, New York, 125 (1986).

20. Hertog, M. G. L., et al., *Nutr. Cancer* 20:21, (1993).

21. Torel, J., Cillard, J. and Cillard, P., *Phytochemistry* 25:383 (1986).

22. Laughton, M. J., et al., *Biochem Pharmacol.* 36:717 (1987).
23. DeWhalley, C. V., et al., *Biochem. Pharmacol.* 39:1743 (1990).
24. Clemetson, C. A. B., *Vitamin C.* CRC Press, Inc., Boca Raton, Florida, p. 101 (1989).

4

Single Substance or Nutritional Team?

THE extra "power" of Pycnogenol comes from the fact that it is not a *simple* bioflavonoid. This chapter explains the composition of Pycnogenol and you will see that it is a specific *blend* of bioflavonoids. The extra potency is not only due to the fact that Pycnogenol contains proanthocyanidins (PACs) which are more soluble and more effective than ordinary bioflavonoids, it is also due to the fact that Pycnogenol contains complex forms of bioflavonoids.

The extract from the maritime pine consists not only of proanthocyanidins, but also of other water-soluble nutrients. These nutrients are building blocks for the production of proanthocyanidins in the living plant and are extracted together with the proanthocyanidins from the pine bark.

In the previous chapter, we discussed flavonoid families including the PACs. Pycnogenol is a mixture of simple bioflavonoids of the PAC family, plus dimers of these simple PACs, plus oligomers of these simple PACs, along with some very useful organic acids such as caffeic acid, cinnamic acid, fumaric acid, gallic acid, vanillic acid, ferulic acid, protocateuhuic acid and just the right amount of taxifolin. You may be able to tell from the names of these nutrients that they are found in other plants. Caffeic acid and ferulic acid are found in parsley and spinach. Caffeic acid is also found in onions and ferulic acid is also found in rhubarb and grapes. Fumaric acid is found in chives and beetroot, and gallic acid is found in eggplant and radish. These minor nutrients of Pycnogenol should not be regarded as a useless ballast beside the powerful proanthocyanidins. These weak organic acids are useful nutrients which contribute to the beneficial effects of Pycnogenol.

What is particularly different about Pycnogenol over simple bioflavonoids and even other simple PACs, is that Pycnogenol includes their *dimers* and *oligomers*. A dimer is formed when two molecules of the same compound join together to form a larger compound, and an oligomer is formed when a small number of molecules join together to form a much larger compound. A polymer is formed when a large number of identical molecules join together to form a much larger molecule. Such very large molecules are rigid and plastic in nature, such as polystyrene (which is formed from linking hundreds of styrene molecules together) and polyurethane (which is formed by linking hundreds of urethane molecules together).

Dimers and oligomers are very small compared to polymers, and have chemical characteristics resembling the basic compound (monomer) from which they are formed. They are well-absorbed and easily transported in blood, yet, they are just different enough so as to produce better antioxidant activity and capillary strengthening. The oligomers are more than just big monomers—they produce their own health benefits. Therefore, it is important that nearly half of the compounds in Pycnogenol are tetramers and higher oligomers.

Perhaps the size relationship can be illustrated with the aid of diagrams. Let the basic bioflavonoid be represented by the letter O. We would then have the symbolic relationships shown in Figure 4.1. The chemical structures of several of the nutrients found in Pycnogenol were presented in Chapter Three.

The differences in size of the molecules accounts for only part of the differences in the biochemistry of the various molecules. However, we cannot show the other relationships diagrammatically. Let us just say that the various fractions of Pycnogenol have been tested as antioxidants, and as anti-inflammatory and anti-edemic compounds, and each fraction has been found to contribute with a specific response profile. The *sum* of all of these actions is what makes Pycnogenol such a unique nutrient.

monomer	O
dimer	O-O
oligomers	O-O-O ,
	O-O-O-O ,
	O-O-O-O-O ,
	O-O-O-O-O-O ,
	O-O-O-O-O-O-O
polymer	O-O-O-O-O-O-O-O-O-O-O-O-O-O-O-O-O-O-O-O-O-O-O
	O-O-O-O-O-O-O-O-O-O-O-O-O-O-O-O-O-O-O-O-O-O-O
	O-O-O-O-O-O-O-O-O-O-O-O-O-O-O-O-O-O-O-O-O-O-O
	O-O-O-O-O-O-O-O-O-O-O-O-O-O-O-O-O-O-O-O-O-O-O
	O-O-O-O-O-O-O-O-O-O-O-O-O-O-O-O-O-O-O-O-O-O-O
	O-O-O-O-O-O-O-O-O-O-O-O-O-O-O-O-O-O-O-O-O-O-O
	O-O-O-O-O-O-O-O-O-O-O-O-O-- etc., etc.

Figure 4.1:
Symbolic size relationships of monomers, dimers,
oligomers and polymers.

In the body, the oligomers are slowly reduced to smaller and smaller molecules until they are dimers and monomers. Thus, when Pycnogenol is first absorbed in the intestine, the entire complex is delivered into the blood. Cells are nourished by basic PACs, PAC dimers, PAC oligomers and organic acids. This is when Pycnogenol is the most effective. As time goes by the original PACs are broken down by normal metabolism, and ''fresh'' PACs replace these as they are liberated from the oligomers as they are metabolized.

At first, there is the power of monomers, dimers and oligomers all working together, but as time passes, the protection of the oligomers decreases because they are converted into monomers, and eventually, when there are no fresh monomers released, their protective effect subsides as they are metabolized.

Oligomers contribute their own activity to the Pycnogenol complex, and as they are metabolized, they contribute again as a "timed-release" of monomers. Thus, Pycnogenol has a unique protection profile—a shorter component due to the actions of all of the components, and a longer action due to the monomers alone. This explains why some benefits of Pycnogenol last for several hours, while other benefits last for days.

Proven in Tests

When reading the clinical studies in this book, three things should be kept in mind. First of all, as scientists, we are reporting the facts as objectively as we can. However, Pycnogenol is not a single nutrient, but a mixture prepared under a commercial process and this fact necessitates that we consider commercial aspects. Pycnogenol is a blend of monomers, dimers, oligomers and organic acids, and this blend must be consistent from production lot to production lot to achieve the wide range of benefits from this supplement. We have determined that indeed this is the case according to our study of production lots from 1991 through 1993.

Secondly, we have strived to assure to the best of our ability, that it is this precise blend that has been used in the tests described in this book. This pine bark extract has been studied and manufactured for decades and as far as we can ascertain, is the product used in the studies presented in this book. Although Dr. Kandaswami has done extensive original research with other *single* bioflavonoids, we are limiting our discussion to the topic of Pycnogenol as much as possible to avoid confusion between various bioflavonoids which do differ markedly in their biochemical actions.

Thirdly, other preparations must be proven in their own clinical studies. One cannot assume that a similar preparation will be equivalent because Nature gives each plant a unique mix of bioflavonoids, and, because of extraction differences, even with the same plant source, the resultant blend may not be identical. Perhaps Dr. Zhao Guochang summarizes this best in his doctoral dissertation:

''Natural extracts contain different complex ingredients. Different extraction methods may obtain different ingredients. Extracts from different sources may contain different components. Even within the same group of flavonoids, molecular structure varies among extracts from different natural sources.''

The molecular structures that represent the proanthocyanidins of Pycnogenol are unique and have proven benefits. These benefits are the subject of this book, so that there is no practical manner in which your authors can avoid stating the facts of commercial production. It is *not* our intent to sound commercial; it *is* our intent to be as accurate as possible in describing the nutrients used and their benefits.

Other flavonoids have merit and specific utility. Today, we know it is important to nourish your body with *all* of the vitamins, and not just concentrate on one vitamin alone. In the future, we may have research indicating that we should supplement our diets with several bioflavonoids. However today, our best advice is to eat a varied and balanced diet having at least five servings of fruits and vegetables a day and, for extra antioxidant protection and healthy blood vessels, consider taking food supplements of Pycnogenol and other antioxidant nutrients.

Since this extract of antioxidant PACs is so good, one wonders how it all came about. Well, the concept may have originated before the sixteenth century, but it took many years of biochemical research and testing to perfect it. The early history of Pycnogenol will be discussed in the next chapter.

5

A History of Pycnogenol
and Other Bioflavonoids

PYCNOGENOL didn't just happen overnight! An infusion of heat and water were used historically (essentially the same extraction used for Pycnogenol today), to extract the beneficial nutrients from the pine bark. It is hard to imagine how North American Indian Medicine Men discovered that a tea brewed from the bark and needles of certain evergreen trees cured scurvy. They did not need to know that they were extracting a small amount of vitamin C and potentiating that with a powerful concentrate of bioflavonoids. Later, chemists would become intrigued with their success and investigate the chemical mechanisms involved. This curiosity led to the discovery of Pycnogenol and many of the benefits of bioflavonoids.

Scurvy is the final result of vitamin C deficiency and leads to death in a short time. When the body becomes so deficient in vitamin C that adequate amounts of collagen cannot be produced to fill the spaces between cells in the capillary walls, the capillaries leak so badly that they hemorrhage. A loathsome disease, scurvy begins with muscle weakness and pain leading to total exhaustion. The joints ache and the slightest effort causes breathlessness. The skin turns dusky and sallow. Depression sets in and rapidly increases in severity. The gums start bleeding, then ulcerate, swell grotesquely and rapidly deteriorate to the point that teeth fall out. The breath becomes extremely foul. The bones become extremely brittle and the jawbone rots. The hemorrhaging, apparent at first as large bruises in the muscles, also occurs in other tissues, leading to lung and kidney failure—then death.

Europeans knew of scurvy before sailors were sent to sea for extended periods with rations that were low in vitamin C. They readily recognized the disease, but had no effective treatment for it. Many thousands of soldiers died of scurvy during long winter campaigns, and many more thousands of citizens died of various plagues and other diseases because they were already weakened with scurvy. Thus, the high prevalence of scurvy in sailors and explorers did not stimulate medical research until centuries passed.

In 1497, when Vasco da Gama sailed from Lisbon to Calicut seeking a new passage to the Indies via Africa's Cape of Good Hope, 100 of the 160-man expedition died of scurvy during the 10-month voyage. In 1519, Magellan set out with five ships to circumnavigate the Earth. He returned three years later with only one ship and 18 original crew members, thanks to scurvy.

French explorer Jacques Cartier's expedition was almost wiped out by scurvy in 1535. In 1536, Hernando Cortes, the conqueror of Mexico, reached Baja California, but had to turn back before reaching California because of the severity of scurvy among his sailors. (The irony is that today California is well-known for its citrus fruits.) In 1577, a Spanish galleon was discovered floating in the Sargasso Sea with all remaining crew members dead from scurvy (some had been buried at sea). In 1593, the English admiral Sir Richard Hawkins estimated that about 10,000 of the sailors under his command had perished from scurvy. Admiral Hawkins came to believe that citrus fruits were protective against scurvy, but his ideas were met with skepticism.

In late 1740, Commodore Anson set sail from England with six ships crewed with 961 sailors (one report listed the crew at 1,500). When he reached Juan Fernandez Island in mid-1741, his crew had dwindled to 335, with more than half succumbing to scurvy. A few years later, in 1747, Scottish physician Dr. James Lind followed up on the concepts promoted by Admiral Hawkins and started his studies that eventually showed citrus fruit juices prevented and cured scurvy. He published his book, *A Treatise on Scurvy,* in 1753.

Captain James Cook led three major Pacific expeditions during 1768–1780 without losing a sailor to scurvy. He brought lots of flavonoid-containing fruits and vegetables, spruce beer made from evergreen needles, vitamin C-containing sauerkraut, and citrus fruits when available. Although English explorer Captain James Cook practiced the teachings of Hawkins and Lind, it took more than 40 years—and 100,000 casualties—to get the British Navy to order daily rations of lime juice to its sailors in 1795. Besides giving them the nickname "limeys," it gave the British Navy superior seaworthiness for long voyages and long watches without relief to thwart Napoleon's attempts to invade England. Unfortunately, it took another 70 years to apply this practice to the civilian merchant marines.

When French researcher, Professor Jacques Masquelier read of the voyages of explorer Jacques Cartier, he came across a passage explaining how a tea prepared from evergreen bark and needles cured scurvy among the sixteenth-century explorers. Professor Masquelier's inquisitive mind led him to consider the biochemistry involved. He knew that there couldn't be very much vitamin C in evergreen needles and essentially none in bark. Why were both bark and needles needed?

Professor Masquelier relates the story as follows: After the discovery of Canada's Gulf of St. Lawrence by Jacques Cartier, ice prevented Cartier and his explorers from leaving the St. Lawrence Waterway in the winter of 1534–35. They landed on the Quebec peninsula to hunt and trap for food as their provisions were dwindling. While on board ship, they were subsisting mostly on salted meat and biscuits. Fresh fruits and vegetables were not to be had.

In December 1534, the explorers were struck down by scurvy. Scurvy had killed 25 of the 110-man crew, and more than 50 others were seriously afflicted and seemed likely to follow suit; only three sailors remained completely unscathed. Most of the remainder were too weak to hunt or even to dig graves for their departed comrades. They could do no better than to bury their comrades in the snow.[1]

Fortunately for Cartier and those still alive, he met a Quebec Indian who told Cartier of a tea brewed from the Anneda tree (or the arbor vitae *Thuja occidentalis*, by another account) that could quickly cure this deadly affliction. The Indian explained that the bark and leaves of the tree must be made into a broth. The liquid must then be drunk and the precipitate applied as a poultice to the swollen joints. Cartier described the Anneda as a large tree with evergreen leaves and a bark that was easy to remove. Cartier immediately tried this remedy on two of his sailors, and they improved so much within a week, that he gave the tea and poultice to all. Feeding the crew tea from the needles and bark of Anneda pine trees cured them of scurvy, and as they say, the rest is history.[1]

The needles contained a small amount of vitamin C, about 50 milligrams per 100 grams of needles, and the bark contained flavonoids which potentiate the antiscorbutic effect of vitamin C. The pine bark tea and its poultice were quickly effective against the horrible scurvy.

More than 400 years later, Professor Jacques Masquelier (at this writing the Dean Emeritus of the Faculty of Materia Medica of the University of Bordeaux, France), was a visiting professor at Quebec University. While at Quebec University, Professor Masquelier researched the flavonols of pine bark, grape skins and various nut shells. He continued this research after he returned to France, and found that the richest source of the most bioavailable and bioactive flavonoids were in the bark of the *Pinus maritima* (or *Pinus pinaster*), which were abundant in Southern France. When Professor Masquelier published his findings in 1966, he believed that the extract was one compound, a leucocy-anidin.[2] He named this compound *Pycnogenol*, which means "substances which deliver condensation products." (Or, more simply, molecules which join together to form larger molecules.) Later, improved analytical instruments showed that the extract was the defined mixture of proan-thocyanidins or PACs.

In 1987, Professor Masquelier patented Pycnogenol for "preventing and fighting the harmful biological effects of free radicals."[3] Professor Masquelier licensed his patent to Horphag Research Ltd. of Guernsey in the U.K., who continue to support international research and the development of Pycnogenol.

REFERENCES

1. Masquelier, Jacques, "Pycnogenols: Recent advances in the therapeutic activity of procyanidins" in *Natural Products as Medicinal Agents* (Beal, J. L. and Reinhard, E., eds.) Hippok-rates Verlag Stuttgart p. 343–56 (1981). Supplement of *Planta Medica, Journal of Medicinal Plant Research and Journal of Natural Products,* Lloydia.

2. Masquelier, Jacques, and Claveau, Pierre, *Naturaliste Canada* 93:345-8 (1966).

3. Masquelier, Jacques, Plant extract with a proanthocyanidins content as therapeutic agent having radical scavenging effect and use thereof. U.S. Patent No. 4,698,360.

6

Allergies, Histamine and
Help from Pycnogenol

IN preparation for this book, Dr. Passwater visited Finland, Germany, France, the Netherlands and the United Kingdom to meet many Pycnogenol researchers and physicians from those and other European countries. It was surprising to learn that most of the European physicians encountered reported that Pycnogenol was their first recommendation for hay fever and related allergies. What do these physicians know that American doctors have yet to learn? Well, it seems that in Europe, physicians are not so dependent on drug companies and their salespeople. European physicians prefer to use the most effective substance with the least adverse effects. In the case of Pycnogenol and hay fever, it is their opinion that Pycnogenol is extremely effective, safe and available at a lower cost than synthetic drugs.

How can a nutrient help control allergy? It has long been known that many bioflavonoids can control allergies, some better than others. An allergy, technically classified as an "immediate-type hypersensitivity," is the body's altered response to a chemical or material. Normally these do not cause a noticeable reaction, but some people become sensitive to certain materials which then are termed *allergens*. In allergen-sensitive persons, the allergens stimulate the production of immunoglobulin E (IgE) by B-lymphocytes. IgE then may bind to mast cells in tissues and basophils in the blood. The binding of IgE to these cells activates the enzyme calcium ATPase which opens calcium channels through cell membranes. Such activated mast cells and basophils, in turn, pump calcium into the cells (into the cell cytosol) which causes the release of histamine and other chemicals from storage granules. In Chapter Three, we mentioned that flavonoids participate in calcium ion translocation. Flavonoids also increase calcium ion export from the cell cytoplasm, reducing ATP consumption for translocation of a given quantity of cytoplasmic calcium ions.

There are other mechanisms that increase the release of histamine in addition to allergen activation, but we are only concerned with allergies in this chapter. Allergy and asthma both involve histamine release, but asthma is more reliant on leukotriene and prostaglandin ratios, whereas allergy is primarily mediated by histamine.

In the United States particularly, allergies are often treated with antihistamines. Antihistamines are also widely used to suppress the running noses of the common cold. Antihistamines work by interfering with the binding of histamine to cells after its release. Pycnogenol and some other bioflavonoids act to *prevent* histamine release in the first place, thereby reducing all adverse effects of histamine, not just interfering with their effects on target cells. The implication readily noticed by European physicians is that flavonoids, especially Pycnogenol, are a better approach to allergy and asthma management than antihistamines.

Another way in which Pycnogenol may reduce histamine availability is by increasing its uptake and storage into granules. Flavonoids can help regulate the production of the enzyme cyclic-AMP phosphodiesterase. This increases cyclic-AMP levels in mast cells and basophils and thus increase the storage of histamine into granules, where the histamine cannot bother other cells until it is released through *degranulation*. (Degranulation is the process during which granules break apart, release their contents and thus, disappear.)

We will discuss the inflammation process in the next chapter, but certainly, inflammation is one of the miseries caused by allergies and colds. Several antioxidant nutrients can decrease inflammation because the inflammation process involves free-radical production. Some antioxidants, including some flavonoids, also normalize lipoxygenase activity which controls leukotriene production.

In 1985, Dr. H. Kakegawa and colleagues reported that catechine and the dimeric proanthocyanidine inhibit the degranulation of mast cells (*Chem. Pharm. Bull.* 33:5079). Degranulation of mast cells would release not only histamine, but all of the mediators of the allergy response.

Dr. David White of the University of Nottingham, England, has shown that Pycnogenol normalizes the activity of the enzyme histidine decarboxylase. This enzyme simply removes a portion of the amino acid histidine to create histamine. Figure 6.1 illustrates the effect of Pycnogenol on histidine decarboxylase activity.

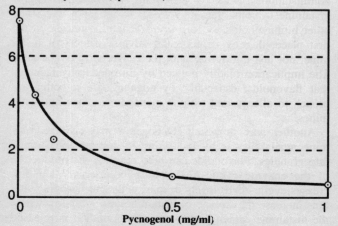

radioactivity release (dpm × 100)

Pycnogenol (mg/ml)

Figure 6.1: Inhibition of histamine formation

7

Pycnogenol Protects the Capillaries

MOST people think of the blood vessel system as arteries and smaller arterioles that carry blood from the heart to the organs, veins and smaller venules that carry blood back to the heart from the organs, and capillaries that link arteries and veins together. This is essentially correct, but it misses the point. Arteries and veins are merely pipes or tubes through which blood flows. Capillaries, on the other hand, are where all the action takes place. While it is necessary to transport blood to where it is needed, this does no good unless the blood components can reach the cells.

The sole function of the circulatory system is to exchange nutrients for waste products. The heart merely pumps the blood and the arteries and veins merely carry the blood. What is important but usually overlooked is that the capillaries allow the cells to live by exchanging nutrients for wastes.

Pycnogenol protects capillaries in three ways. Unlike multi-layered arteries and veins, capillaries are composed of a single cell layer. These cells are reinforced with collagen, a somewhat elastic protein fiber. Also, the "intercellular cement" or ground substance—the material that fills the space between cells—consists largely of collagen. Vitamin C is needed for the production of collagen, therefore, vitamin C's helpers, the bioflavonoids, are also important. We've already discussed three ways in which Pycnogenol helps protect vitamin C; this is the first way in which Pycnogenol helps maintain a healthy capillary system. However, the bioflavonoids of Pycnogenol have a second function in that they adhere to collagen, offering additional protection.

If the intercellular substance is damaged, there is a microscopic hole in the capillary which becomes a channel for a leak. The thin wall of the cells can be damaged by free-radical attack and also leak. The third way in which Pycnogenol protects capillaries is by protecting cells against free-radical attack.

Capillary resistance and permeability are improved by Pycnogenol.[1] Several European medical studies show that Pycnogenol improves peripheral circulation, restores lost capillary activity, and strengthens weak blood vessels.[2-6] By reducing capillary fragility, Pycnogenol helps prevent bruising and improves varicose veins.[7,8] In addition, Pycnogenol reduces venous insufficiency, reduces restless legs and diminishes lower leg blood volume.[9,10]

Pycnogenol also protects the membranes of red blood cells so that they remain flexible and easily squeezed through the very narrow capillaries, one at a time. The membranes of red blood cells have a high degree of flexibility which allows the red blood cells to swell or to shrink according to the concentrations of electrolytes in the blood. Also, red blood cells must change their shape to ellipsoids when they are pressed through small capillaries with a high blood flow, and then be able to spring back quickly to their normal round shape when the blood velocity slows in the larger blood vessels.

Professor Artmann of the Department of Physical Engineering of Fachhochschule Aachen in Germany demonstrated in a series of experiments that Pycnogenol stabilizes red blood cells and maintains their proper flexibility. Pycnogenol not only stabilizes the leaky blood vessels by the proper cross linking of collagen, it stabilizes the red blood cells so that it is harder for them to squeeze through tiny leaks in blood vessels.

Capillaries are important because they carry nutrients to cells and carry away waste. Capillaries must be permeable enough to allow fluids to seep out of the capillaries, mix with the fluid that surrounds all of the cells, and then re-enter the capillaries. If the capillaries are *too* permeable, boo much fluid and protein seeps out, resulting in edema. Red blood cells may also seep out, causing bruising and red spots.

A key component of all blood vessels, including capillaries, is that they contain elastic strands of collagen. Pycnogenol prevents substances from damaging these elastic strands and making the blood vessels more permeable. In other words, Pycnogenol restores the elasticity of collagen, and, in so doing, restores the impermeability of blood vessel walls. European studies through the years have shown that Pycnogenol strengthens capillaries, as has been measured as increased capillary resistance to an applied vacuum. (This measures the force that the capillaries can withstand before leaking fluid and red blood cells.)

Scientists also measure capillary integrity directly by measuring permeability by the amount of dye that leaks through the capillary. This leakage can also be measured by placing a constriction around a part of an extremity and taking blood samples from both sides of the constriction over a period of time. The blood samples are then analyzed for proteins that have leaked and accumulated.

The vacuum procedure is comparatively easy because it is noninvasive. A measured suction (partial vacuum) is applied to the skin and the suction force is increased until red spots appear on the skin surface. There are instruments to perform this test which help standardize this procedure and make measurements a routine matter.

This test has shown that Pycnogenol produces a greater and longer improvement in capillary resistance (resistance to leakage) than most bioflavonoids. Nearly all bioflavonoids produce a moderate, short-term improvement. This is said to be a *monophasic* effect. However, Pycnogenol produces an additional effect which is stronger and longer-lasting. This response is said to be *diphasic*. This longer effect has been measured as lasting up to 168 hours, and is thought to be due to Pycnogenol's sparing effect on vitamin C and its adherence to collagen. Citrus bioflavonoids and hesperidin do not produce the diphasic effect.

In 1965, Professor Jacques Masquelier gave 45 persons suffering from venous or capillary disorders a single 100 milligram supplement of Pycnogenol and 72 hours later they were found to have increased capillary resistance by 140 percent.[8]

In another study, 31 persons were given 90 milligrams of Pycnogenol daily for two months. Their capillary resistance improved markedly. The study subjects reported that their edema had vanished and their legs felt invigorated.

In a study involving guinea pigs (like humans, one of the few animals who do not produce vitamin C in their bodies), 5 milligrams of Pycnogenol per kilogram of body weight increased their capillary resistance an average of 82 percent. Capillary resistance was measured in guinea pigs after 10 days of oral administration of 1,500 milligrams of Pycnogenol daily. There was nearly a 300 percent improvement, which was found to be highly statistically significant.

Dr. Miklos Gabor of Szent-Gyorgyi Medical University in Hungary has researched capillary resistance and permeability for about forty years and is considered the world's expert on the relationship between flavonoids and capillaries. He has researched the effect of Pycnogenol on capillaries since 1979. Dr. Gabor has found that Pycnogenol protects capillaries against many of the stimuli that can cause an inflammatory response. Dr. Kandaswami has followed the research of Dr. Gabor for many years and has quoted from Dr. Gabor's research in his own original research. Dr. Passwater visited with Dr. Gabor in Europe to learn firsthand of his latest research for this book.

Perhaps it would be more interesting if part of our actual conversations were shared with you. Let us, with the permission of the publisher of *Whole Foods* magazine, excerpt portions of an interview with Dr. Gabor that appeared there.[11]

QUESTION: Dr. Gabor, you have designed a simple portable petechiometer to measure the degree of *petechiae* [small hemorrhages appearing as red spots] formation permitted by weak capillaries. If capillaries are too permeable, they are no longer a barrier to infection. Dr. Gabor, what has your research shown in regards to Pycnogenol and capillary permeability?

GABOR: I have studied the effect of water-soluble flavone derivatives (proanthocyanidins and hesperidin-methylchalcone) on the vascular wall resistance. Pycnogenol increases pathologically low capillary resistance, decreases an enhanced capillary permeability and improves circulation. As I explain in a report that is in press (*Scripta Phlebologica*, 1994), the anti-inflammatory action of proanthocyanidins may be based on increasing the capillary resistance, but additional factors should be taken into consideration. The antioxidant action of Pycnogenol has been reported; it is able to scavenge superoxide radicals, it reduces UV-B radiation-induced cytotoxicity of fibroblasts, and inhibits lipid peroxidation.

Free radicals and other reactive oxygen species are formed at the sites of inflammation and contribute to tissue damage. The scavenging effect of Pycnogenol for radicals correlates with its anti-inflammatory activity. Pycnogenol may also act by inhibiting lipoxygenase and cyclooxygenase.

QUESTION: Does this research mean that Pycnogenol would be of help to people having fragile capillaries that might result in problems such as bleeding gums, floaters caused by bleeding into the retina, glaucoma, bleeding kidneys, and stroke? Also, I have seen European studies that show that Pycnogenol is a nutritional adjunct that helps against varicose veins, heavy menstrual bleeding, hemorrhoids and the complications of diabetes.

GABOR: I have not personally conducted clinical trials on these conditions, but I think the answer is obvious. Capillary health is compromised in all of these conditions, and Pycnogenol acts to improve capillary health by improving their bioflavonoid nourishment. The chief use of flavonoids is in the treatment of disease states characterized by capillary bleeding associated with increased capillary fragility. These include degenerative vascular disease, allergic states, and various other disorders. The purpose of nourishment with Pycnogenol is to reduce the incidence of capillary hemorrhage and thus to prevent its consequences. Our own experimental studies concern above all the capillary resistance-increasing action or anti-inflammatory effect of Pycnogenol.

These data stimulated us to carry out capillary resistance determinations in spontaneous hypertension rats. As the results reveal, pathologically low values were observed in the large majority of the experimental animals. This study revealed that the pathologically low vascular wall resistance of the spontaneous hypertension rats can be normalized with Pycnogenol.

It has long been known that the capillary resistance is pathologically decreased in a considerable proportion of hypertensive subjects (Griffith and Lindauer, 1944; Kuchmeister and Scharfe, 1950; Gough, 1962; Davis and Landau, 1970; etc.). Special mention should be made of the observation that, if hypertension is associated with a low capillary resistance, the incidence of cerebral insults (apoplexy or stroke) and retinal hemorrhage is essentially higher. It was established by Paterson (1940) that capillary rupture accompanied by intimal bleeding plays a role in the mechanism of cerebral arterial thrombosis. He assumed that, at the intracapillary pressure resulting from the high blood pressure, the capillary fragility (which is enhanced for various reasons) is responsible for the intimal rupture of the cerebral capillaries. These data stimulated us to carry out capillary resistance determinations in spontaneous hypertension rats. As the results reveal, pathologically low values were observed in the large majority of the experimental animals.

This fact should be of interest to hypertensive persons as the capillary resistance is pathologically decreased in a considerable proportion of hypertensive persons. This is why hypertensives have greater risk of stroke and retinal hemorrhage. It is not the high blood pressure that was bursting the blood vessels, but it is the decreased capillary resistance and increased permeability that is the cause. The blood vessels do not have to burst. Our studies reveal that pathologically low vascular wall resistance can be normalized by treatment with Pycnogenol.

QUESTION: For many years you have been studying the effects of flavonoids on the capillary resistance of psoriatic patients. Can you make any conclusions yet?

GABOR: The capillary resistance of psoriatic patients is significantly lower than that of healthy persons. Pycnogenol tends to restore normal capillary resistance in these psoriatic patients. I have not conducted a clinical trial of the effect of Pycnogenol, but my observations and anecdotal evidence supports the premise that Pycnogenol is very useful in controlling psoriasis.

QUESTION: How do the bioflavonoids help capillaries maintain their proper resistance and permeability?

GABOR: I have been studying the actions of the flavonoids in elevating capillary resistance since the early 1950s and I have published a detailed survey of the results of all of the relevant research in 1974. I have observed that Pycnogenol improves the capillary resistance within two hours and maintains it longer than eight hours. However, just as with inflammation, we still have a lot to learn about the "how" part.

QUESTION: What has your research shown about bioflavonoids (especially Pycnogenol) and inflammation?

GABOR: I have recently published that Pycnogenol inhibits inflammation in a dose-dependent manner.[12] Pycnogenol, sophoricoside and fisetin are the most effective flavonoids against inflammation that I have tested.

The mechanisms at play involve the inhibition of several chemical mediators, including histamine, prostaglandins, 5-hydroxytryptamine and kinins. Also, these flavonoids can block undesirable actions of lipoxygenase and cyclooxygenase. The actions of Pycnogenol against inflammation are different than those of rutin, hesperidin and the citroflavonoids.

Professor Gabor's discussion of his research on capillaries provides us with an excellent introduction to the topics of inflammation, edema and varicose veins for the following chapter.

REFERENCES

1. Cahn, J. and Borzeix, M. G., "Etude de L'administration D'oligomeres procyanidoliques (OPC) chez le rat." Extrait de La Semaine des Hospitaux de Paris 59 27–28:2031–4 (1983).

2. Dartenus et al., *Bordeaux Med.* 13:903 (1980).

3. Beylot et al., *Gaz. Med. de France* 87:2919 (1980).

4. Biard et al., *Medicine Prat.* 786:62 (1980).

5. Baracco et al., *Gaz Med. de France* 88:2035 (1981).

6. Laparra et al., *Expertise Pharmacologique* (1978).

7. Lagru et al., *Vie Med.* 1299 (1980).

8. Feine-Haake, G., "A new therapy for venous diseases." Zeitschrift fur Allgemeinmedizin 839 (June 30, 1975).

9. Blazso, G. and Gabor, M., "Oedema-inhibiting effect of procyanidin." Acta Physiologica Scientiarum Hungaricae, Tomus 56(2):235–40 (1980).

10. Schmidtke, I. and Schoop, W., Das hydrostatische odem und seine medikamentose beeinflussung. Schweizerische gesellschaft fur phebologie. Jahrestagung 1984. "Die Objektivierung der Wirkung von Venepharmaka." *Lenzerheide* (Jan. 19/21, 1984).

11. An interview with Dr. Miklos Gabor by Richard A. Passwater, Ph.D. *Whole Foods* (scheduled for September 1994).

12. Gabor, Miklos and Razga, "Pycnogenol inhibits inflammation in a dose-dependent manner." *Acta. Physiol. Hung.* 77:197–207 (1991).

8

Inflammation, Edema and Varicose Veins

AN *inflammation* is a tissue's response to irritation, injury or infection. Inflammation is marked by localized heat, swelling, pain, possibly redness and loss of function. This includes such symptoms as the swollen and red nose of hay fever, headaches, the swelling following twisting an ankle, or the swelling and redness of a boil. The swelling is due to *edema* which is a collection of fluid in the spaces between cells of the tissues. This fluid can collect because it spills from capillaries. In a severe injury, the capillary may burst, spilling its contents before the body seals of the capillary. Strong capillaries can resist minor injuries, and sports teams that take bioflavonoids have fewer incapacitating injuries and even then have their players back in action faster than normal.

However, this chapter is not about sports injuries. It is about the inflammation of arthritis, allergies, infection, sunburn, the edema of congestive heart disease and even about halting the formation of varicose veins. Inflammation can occur because bioflavonoid deficiency can make capillaries porous and free radicals and other oxygen species can initiate the inflammatory response. Pycnogenol has been shown to strengthen capillaries and quench free-radical attack.

Varicose Veins and Venous Insufficiency

After the blood is collected again by the capillaries and returned to the veins, it must be pumped back to the heart.

But by now, the pressure of the heart beat has been diminished as the blood has diffused through the capillaries. The veins have a built-in pump that is powered by the action of our skeletal muscles.

The large muscles of the legs help power the blood the long way back through the veins. This system is called the "muscle-vein" pump. Every time we use a large muscle, that muscle simultaneously presses on veins, which helps push the blood along. The veins have one-way valves, which prevent the blood from falling back due to the pull of gravity when there is no muscle contractions.

When we are inactive for long periods of time, the muscle pump is not active. As a result, blood volume increases in the veins and the pressure also rises. The one-way valves can give in allowing gravity to pull the blood. This results in edema, swelling and pain. Over time, this produces varicose veins and/or hemorrhoids.

Dr. F. Feine-Haake of Horphag Research, Ltd. studied the benefit of 30 milligrams of Pycnogenol given three times a day (a total of 90 mg) on 100 persons having varicose veins. Eighty percent showed a clear improvement. Additionally, among the 40 individuals in that group who had nightly leg cramps, 90 percent reported that the Pycnogenol prevented the cramping.

Another study involved 110 persons having nocturnal leg cramps or pain. They were given 90 milligrams of Pycnogenol daily for five days, and then half this amount for nine days. The symptoms disappeared completely in 50 percent and were significantly relieved in another 31 percent.

Edema

Italian scientists studied the effect of Pycnogenol on venous congestion in the legs (leg edema). The study involved 40 subjects consisting of 13 men and 27 women between the ages of 34 and 74, having an average age of 60 years. The subjects were randomly divided into two groups. One group served as the control group and received a placebo supplement that appeared identical to the Pycnogenol supplement, only it contained an inactive substance. The other group received 300 milligrams of Pycnogenol daily for 60 days.

All of those taking the Pycnogenol had relief from at least some of the symptoms. There was a decrease in the weight of the lower limbs in 11 percent of those receiving Pycnogenol after 30 days, and in 33 percent after 60 days.[1]

The swelling disappeared in 26 percent of those taking the Pycnogenol after 30 days, and in 63 percent after 60 days (circumference measured above the ankle before and after test). Pain in the lower limbs was totally relieved in 33 percent of those taking Pycnogenol after 30 days, and in 67 percent after 60 days.

How Pycnogenol Protects Capillaries and Reduces Inflammation and Edema

During the inflammation process, the enzymes collagenase and elastase are released which damage the skin proteins collagen and elastin. Studies have shown that Pycnogenol bioflavonoids bind to these skin proteins and protect them against degradation by the collagenase and elastase enzymes.[2-4]

Another damaging enzyme is hyaluronidase, a mucopolysaccharide-splitting enzyme which is related to increase permeability of capillaries and other blood vessels, as well as to inflammation. Two of the bioflavonoids of Pycnogenol, catechin and one of the PAC dimers (proanthocyanidin B-2) inhibit hyaluronidase. Thus, Pycnogenol protects hyaluronic acid, a basic constituent of connective tissue.[5]

Still another damaging agent is the reactive oxygen species hypochlorous acid. Hypochlorous acid (HOC1) is produced when chloride ions are oxidized by the enzyme myeloperoxidase in the presence of hydrogen peroxide. It can be formed at the sites of inflammation. Hypochlorous acid can attack many biological molecules, but one important target for our discussion here is alpha-antiproteinase. Alpha-antiproteinase is a major inhibitor of elastase. When hypochlorous acid damages alpha-antiproteinase, elastase production is no longer inhibited and elastase is released to damage tissues. Pycnogenol can neutralize hypochlorous acid and thus help keep elastase in check.[6]

Of course, elastin and collagen are key skin proteins. Let's look at how Pycnogenol protects the skin next.

REFERENCES

1. Spartera, Carlo, Report, Univ. Aquila (June 16, 1989).

2. Masquelier, Jacques, *Parfums Cosmetiques Aromes* 95:92 (1990).

3. Kuttan, R., Donnelly, Patricia V. and Di Ferrante, N. "Collagen treated with catechin becomes resistant to the action of mammalian collagenase." *Experientia* 37:221 (1981).

4. Tixier, J. M., Godeau, G., Robert, A. M. and Hornbeck, W., "Evidence by in vivo and in vitro studies that binding of Pycnogenols to elastin affects its rate of degradation by elastases." *Biochem. Pharm.* 33:3933–9 (1984).

5. Kakegawa, Hisao et al., "Inhibitory effects of tannins on hyaluronidase activation and on the degranulation from rat mesentery mast cells." *Chem. Pharm. Bull.* 33:5079–82 (1985).

6. Personal communication between R. Passwater and Professor Peter Rohdewald, Ph.D. of the University of Muenster, Germany.

9

The Super Skin Nutrient

UNTIL now, we have discussed the importance of Pycnogenol to the condition of the proteins collagen and elastin in terms of blood vessel health. This is quite important to those having capillary disorders. However, Pycnogenol can be of great benefit to healthy people as well. Pycnogenol's protection of these proteins also means better and younger-looking skin. Now we got your attention didn't we!

As researchers, we are interested in preventing the diseases of age and even slowing the aging process itself. One of the effects of aging that concerns many people is the change in skin texture and appearance. Aging causes the skin to become thinner and more transparent. The subcutaneous layer loses fat and the skin sags. And, unfortunately, elastic skin fibers lose their resilience.

Well-nourished, healthy skin is radiant and youthful. Pycnogenol is an important part of optimally nourishing your skin. Pycnogenol isn't an essential nutrient for skin, but it does offer important protection and revitalization. Pycnogenol will not make old skin new, but it will improve the elasticity and appearance of your skin.

Collagen, one of the body's most ubiquitous proteins, is the primary component of the skin. An interlacing of collagen fibers with a fine net of elastin (an essential component of connective tissue) gives skin its strength, elasticity and smoothness. Pycnogenol reactivates damaged collagen and elastin and protects them against further attack by free radicals and degrading enzymes, the elastases and collagenase.[1-4]

Pycnogenol binds to collagen fibers and realigns them to a more youthful, undamaged form. This protective action of Pycnogenol helps to prevent the early facial wrinkles that occur due to skin inelasticity.

One could even consider Pycnogenol to be an oral cosmetic to help keep skin smooth and elastic. Actually, it was dermatological and phlebological disorders that started Dr. Jacques Masquelier of Bordeaux University on the road to researching Pycnogenol. He treated 45 patients having eczema, ulcerated varicose veins and related disorders.

When collagen fibers are soaked in water for 24 hours with a weight attached, their strength can be measured relative to the length that the fiber is stretched. When Pycnogenol is added to the water, the collagen fibers decrease in length proportional to the amount of Pycnogenol added. This decrease represents an increase in collagen strength. The weight of the collagen fibers also increases after incubation in the Pycnogenol solution. Bioflavonoids such as rutin and hesperidin do not have this strengthening effect on collagen.

The fragmentation of elastin fibers during aging can be attributed to an imbalance between the elastase enzyme and its natural inhibitors. When the enzyme elastase is introduced in the dermal layer of skin in laboratory animals, the degradation of the elastin fibers can be observed with a microscope. If the animals are given Pycnogenol first, this degradation is reduced by up to 70 percent.[1,2]

Studies at Baylor College of Medicine in Texas show that the catechin bioflavonoids bind tightly with skin collagen so as to prevent enzyme degradation.[3]

Besides the protection provided when Pycnogenol binds to collagen and elastin, it provides additional protection to skin with its free-radical quenching ability. Healthy skin needs to be protected against damaging ultraviolet radiation from the sun. Over exposure to sunlight causes premature wrinkling. UV radiation can produce a variety of dermatological effects in humans including erythema, photosensitivity, immunological alterations, photoaging, and carcinogenesis. UV-B is considered to be the portion of the UV spectrum primarily responsible for the deleterious effect of solar UV radiation.

One possible mechanism underlying UV-B radiation-induced cell damage is oxidative stress. Oxidative stress is a cellular situation characterized by an elevation in the steady-state concentration of free radicals and other reactive oxygen species. Oxidative stress occurs if the balance between the cellular antioxidant defenses and the mechanisms triggering oxidative conditions is impaired.

Topical sunscreens are your first line of protection, but the skin also needs free-radical fighters in your skin to protect against the UV-released radicals from the UV rays that do penetrate the sunscreen.

Pycnogenol makes an excellent external and internal "sunscreen." Dr. Antti Holevi Arstilla, Chairman of the Department of Cell Biology at the University of Jyvaeskylae in Jyvaeskylae, Finland reported that in an *in vitro* (test tube) experiment in which human skin cells were exposed to UV energy, Pycnogenol provided excellent protection, clearly better than equal amounts of vitamin E. Vitamin E's protection leveled off, whereas Pycnogenol's protection remained dose-dependent over a wider range.[5]

In typical experiments of this type, sunlight will kill about 50 percent of the skin cells. When adequate Pycnogenol is added, about 85 percent of the skin cells survive.[5]

To measure the effect of Pycnogenol as an external sunscreen, Dr. Peter Rohdewald and a colleague exposed skin with varying concentrations of Pycnogenol ointment to 30 minutes of controlled UV energy. The results compared favorably to those of other sunscreens, they reported. The forearms were exposed to UV-B radiation also and protection could be seen with a Pycnogenol concentration as low as 0.75 percent.

This is important, not only in preventing premature wrinkling due to overexposure to sunlight, but for preventing skin cancer as well. Let's let Dr. Arstila explain the importance of his research.

ARSTILA: Zhao Guochang and I thought that since skin fibroblasts (cells found in growing tissue) have important functions in skin dermis, that it would be important to study the effects of UV-B on skin fibroblasts and then find ways of protecting the fibroblasts.

QUESTION: Does Pycnogenol protect skin from UV damage?

ARSTILA: Yes. Pycnogenol reduced UV-B radiation-induced cytotoxicity and lipid peroxidation in a manner proportional to the amount of Pycnogenol present. Our studies indicate that UV-B radiation induces oxidative stress in cultured human skin fibroblasts, that UV-B induced oxidative injuries are not reduced by dl-alpha-tocopherol but are reduced by Pycnogenol, and that Pycnogenol scavenges superoxide radicals in vitro.

QUESTION: Isn't Pycnogenol a good nutrient for skin anyway because it facilitates the production of the skin protein collagen?

ARSTILA: Yes, through its protection and sparing of vitamin C, it does aid collagen development. But, perhaps of greater interest, is that it improves the beneficial cross-linking between the amino acids of the fibers that give skin its flexibility and strength, while preventing the undesirable cross-linking between the amino acids that ages skin like leather. The nutrients of Pycnogenol have a great affinity for skin proteins and that helps protect them against free radicals and other reactive oxygen species.

REFERENCES

1. Masquelier, J., Dumon, M. C., and Dumas, J., "Stabilisation du collagene par des oligomeres procyanidoliques." *Acta Therapeutica* 7:101–5 (1981).
2. Tixier, J. M., Godeau, G., Robert, A. M. and Hornebeck, W., "Evidence by in vivo and in vitro studies that binding of

Pycnogenols to elastin affects its rate of degradation by elastases.'' *Biochem. Pharmacol.* 33(24):3933–9 (1984).

3. Kuttan, R., Donnelly, Patricia V. and Di Ferrante, N., ''Collagen treated with catechin becomes resistant to the action of mammalian collagenase.'' *Experientia* 37:221–3 (1981).

4. Kakegawa, H., et al., *Chem. Pharm. Bull.* 33:5079 (1985).

5. Arstila, Antti Holevi and Guochang, Zhao, personal communications and the doctoral thesis of Zhao Guochang. University of Jyvaeskylae, Finland (1993).

10

Help for Heart Disease from Antioxidants

PERHAPS everyone has now seen one of the studies linking the consumption of the bioflavonoids in red wine with lower rates of heart disease.[1,2] As early as 1957, it had been shown that wine protected animals on a high-cholesterol diet.[3] Red wine is rich in bioflavonoids and contains a moderate amount of alcohol. Dr. John Folts of the University of Wisconsin Medical School has presented evidence that it is the bioflavonoids in wine that provides the protective effect, rather than the alcohol.[4] Other studies indicate that in moderate drinking, it is the alcohol's action on lipoproteins that is protective.[2]

Still other studies have linked the consumption of dietary bioflavonoids including apples and tea with reduced rates of heart disease. A recent study from the Netherlands showed an inverse correlation between dietary flavonoid intake and the incidence of coronary heart disease.[5] The individuals with the lowest dietary intake of flavonoids had the highest incidence of heart disease. It is striking to note that the relative incidence of heart disease among men who had the highest intake of flavonoids was only a third of those who had the lowest intake of flavonoids. The results were the same even after adjustments for age, body fat, smoking, blood cholesterol level, blood pressure, physical activity, coffee consumption, and the intake of calories, vitamin C, vitamin E, beta-carotene and dietary fiber.

The First Part of Pycnogenol's Protection

When Dr. David White of the Faculty of Medicine at the University of Nottingham, England gave his lecture at the International Conference on Pycnogenol Research in 1990, he may have provided the final clue needed to solve the heart disease mystery.[6]

Many studies have now shown that cholesterol in the bloodstream becomes lodged in artery walls and begin to clogs arteries *only* when their transporters, the lipoproteins, have chemically combined with oxygen to turn rancid. The damaged lipoproteins are called *oxidized LDL* and their role is discussed further at the end of this chapter.

Harvard researchers have been studying the role of anti-oxidant nutrients in preventing heart disease for some time. In the 1980s, several researchers were independently becoming aware that antioxidant nutrients were reducing the risk of heart disease. In 1990, Dr. Charles Hennekens of Harvard reported that beta-carotene reduced the incidence of heart attacks in half in a double-blind, placebo-controlled clinical trial.

Also, Harvard researchers reported two studies in the *New England Journal of Medicine* in 1993 showing vitamin E supplements significantly reduced heart disease.[7,8] One study is called the Nurses Study and the other is referred to as the Health Professionals Study. Prior to the final published reports in the *New England Journal of Medicine*, various aspects of the ongoing studies were released.

The Harvard researchers studied the diets of 87,245 nurses over more than eight years. They found that women who take supplements of more than 100 IU of vitamin E daily have 36 percent fewer heart attacks than those who consume less than 30 IU daily.

The Harvard researchers also found that women who consumed 25,000 IU of beta-carotene daily had 40 percent less stroke and 22 percent fewer heart attacks than those women who consumed less than 10,000 IU of beta-carotene daily. The researchers did not study Pycnogenol, but our point is that the antioxidant protection of LDL is critical in preventing heart disease, and that Pycnogenol is synergistic with the other antioxidant nutrients and has been shown to be a very powerful and effective antioxidant in its own right.

In the *New England Journal of Medicine* report on the Nurses Study, the results showed that as compared with women in the lowest fifth of vitamin E intake, those in the top fifth had a relative risk of major coronary disease of 0.66 (a 34 percent reduction) after adjusting for age and smoking. Further adjustments for a variety of other coronary risk factors and nutrients, including some antioxidants (but not flavonoids), had little effect on the results. The researchers concluded, ''These data . . . suggest the use of vitamin E supplements is associated with a reduced risk of coronary heart disease.''

In the *New England Journal of Medicine* report on health professionals, the results showed that after controlling for age and several coronary disease risk factors, there was a lower risk of coronary disease among men with higher intakes of vitamin E. For men consuming more than 60 IU per day of vitamin E, the multivariate relative risk was 0.64 (a 36 percent reduction) as compared with those consuming less than 7.5 IU per day. As compared with men who did not take vitamin E supplements, men who took at least 100 IU per day for at least two years had a multivariate relative risk of coronary heart disease of 0.63 (a 37 percent reduction).

The Harvard researchers concluded, ''These data . . . provide evidence of an association between a high intake of vitamin E and a lower risk of coronary heart disease in men.''

The Harvard studies agree well with a 1974 study by Dr. Passwater.[9] In studying 17,894 persons between the ages of 50 and 98 in 1974, it was found that heart disease dropped dramatically among those taking vitamin E over a long period of time. Further, the length of time vitamin

E was taken was more important than the amount, Passwater's research showed.

This correlates well with the finding of Dr. Fred Gey of the University of Bern in Switzerland showing that vitamin E deficiency is the single most important risk factor in predicting heart disease incidence.[10]

Professor Hermann Esterbauer's group at the University of Graz in Austria has reported that the ''oxidation of polyunsaturated fatty acids in LDL is preceded by a sequential depletion of antioxidants.'' [11] Oxidation of LDL can begin only when these antioxidants have been depleted. Various antioxidant nutrients have their specific place in their affinity for oxygen-free radicals. This ''pecking order'' results in various antioxidant lines of defense against these reactive agents.

What we now know is that vitamin E is the last defense against the oxygen-free radicals that damage the cholesterol carriers. The carriers, low-density lipoproteins, normally contain vitamin E which protects them from oxidation. However, the vitamin E can be quickly destroyed during exposure to many oxygen molecules or oxygen-species free radicals. Vitamin C can help by regenerating this ''spent'' vitamin E.

This leads to the importance of Pycnogenol. The Pycnogenol compounds protect vitamin C, thus, they become one of the body's first lines of defense against heart disease. Other antioxidant nutrients such as beta-carotene, thiols, coenzyme Q-10 and selenium contribute to this defense as well.

Our point is that the antioxidant protection of LDL is critical in preventing heart disease, and that Pycnogenol is not only synergistic with the other antioxidant nutrients; it has been shown to be a very powerful and effective antioxidant in its own right.

The Second Part of Pycnogenol's Protection

The path to a heart attack is a two-step process. First

"foam cells" (macrophages filled with oxidized-LDL) are produced in the artery wall as we just discussed in a process involving oxidized-LDL. Foam cells may also be produced at damaged sites in the artery lining. These cells promote the infiltration of various substances through the artery wall into its middle layer. Now the artery can be said to be "diseased" as a plaque is formed in the artery interior. As the plaque expands, the wall is pushed out and the opening where the blood flows through is narrowed. Thus, blood flow is decreased to the heart tissue. The narrowed artery also damages the blood platelets passing through, making the blood sticky and encouraging clot formation at the plaque site.

Pycnogenol protects us against heart disease in another way as well. Besides its antioxidant action of protecting LDL from oxidation and its protection of the artery lining, Pycnogenol helps keep the blood platelets from becoming stickier and developing a tendency to unnecessarily clump together. Coupled with Pycnogenol's protection of the artery linings and affinity for collagen fibers in the artery lining, this reduces the undesirable formation of the blood clots that cause coronary thrombosis resulting in myocardial infarction.

The anticlotting factor is especially important. The first action most cardiologists take today is to prescribe aspirin. Now aspirin doesn't lower cholesterol or blood pressure, but studies show that it reduces heart attacks by 30 to 50 percent by reducing blood clotting. Unfortunately, aspirin can reduce the clotting ability so much as to cause bleeding, and it can be an irritant to the gastrointestinal tract that can cause serious bleeding there.

Pycnogenol on the other hand, does not interfere with the enzyme that aspirin interferes with, which results in a longer time required to form a clot. Pycnogenol *protects* the blood platelets and also *prevents* the platelets from adhering to the artery walls. Both of these actions reduce the risk of forming deadly clots.

There is much more to the protective action of Pycnogenol and other antioxidants against heart disease. For more detail, refer to *The New Supernutrition*.[12]

For the Health Professional

When LDL particles become oxidized, it is an entirely different situation than with normal "native" LDL. Oxidized LDL is not taken up by LDL receptors, but, as Dr. Daniel Steinberg of the University of California at San Diego has shown, oxidized LDL is uncontrollably taken up by a scavenger-LDL receptor (acetyl-LDL receptor).[13] The native-LDL receptor is regulated according to the cell's need for cholesterol. When cholesterol needs are met, the cell produces fewer LDL receptors and cholesterol transport into the cell diminishes accordingly.

In the case of oxidized LDL which is taken up by the scavenger receptors of monocytes, there is no regulation of these receptors by cellular cholesterol and, as a result, the scavenger receptors continue to pull oxidized-LDL into the monocyte/macrophage. The monocyte/macrophage becomes cholesterol laden, immobile and appears as a white foam cell trapped in the artery wall. This development attracts other monocytes to the area, and the foam cell formation is extended and invades the artery wall. Thus oxidized LDL becomes a major cause of plaque build-up, independent of the otherwise prerequisite damage to the artery lining. Eventually, a rather complicated structure— the atherosclerotic plaque—develops, consisting of lipids, complex carbohydrates, blood, blood products, fibrous tissue and calcium deposits.

However, endothelial damage is another mechanism that can produce plaque. Damage to the endothelium from high pressure or flow velocity can activate the artery's repair mechanism by summoning monocytes or producing apolipoprotein(a).

Injury to the layer of endothelial cells (which normally form the luminal surface of blood vessel walls) disturbs local vascular homeostasis resulting in platelet deposition, aggregation and release of factors which promote smooth muscle proliferation and eventual fibrosis. The damaged endothelium also becomes permeable to lipoproteins, particularly low density lipoproteins (LDL) and monocytes/macrophages which invade the site of injury.

The collagen-rich connective tissue in artery walls can be protected by Pycnogenol.[14] Studies show that Pycnogenol is protective against early atherosclerosis.[15-18] Pycnogenol reduces histamine production, thereby helping artery linings resist attack by mutagens, oxidized-LDL cholesterol and free radicals.

REFERENCES

1. St. Leger, A. S., Cochrane, A. L. and Moore, H., "Eighteen country study of mortality due to ischemic heart disease," *Lancet* 1017 (May 12, 1979).

2. Gaziano, J. M., Buring, J. E., et al., "Moderate alcohol intake, increased levels of high-density lipoprotein and its subfractions, and decreased risk of myocardial infarction," *New Engl. J. Med.* 329(25):1829–34 (Dec. 16, 1993).

3. Fay-Morgan, A., Brinner, L., Plaa, C. B. and Stone, M. M., "Protective effect of wine in laboratory animals fed a cholesterol-enriched diet," *Amer. J. Physiol.* 189:290 (1957).

4. Demrow, H., Jackson, D. and Folts, J., "French red wine, but not white wine, inhibits in vivo activity and thrombosis in stenosed canine coronary arteries." *Thromb. Haemostas.*, TTHADQ 69(6):587 (1993).

5. Hertog, M. G. L., et al., "Dietary antioxidant flavonoids and the risk of coronary heart disease: The Zutphen Elderly Study," *Lancet* 342:1007–11 (1993).

6. White, David, "Cholesterol and foam cell control with Pycnogenol: the atherosclerosis antidote," The International Conference on Pycnogenol Research, Bordeaux, France, October 4–6, 1990.

7. Stampfer, M. J., Hennekens, C. H., et al., "Vitamin E consumption and the risk of coronary disease in women," *New Engl. J. Med.* 328:1444–9 (1993).

8. Rimm, E. B., Stampfer, M. J., et al., "Vitamin E consumption and the risk of coronary heart disease in men," *New Engl. J. Med.* 328:1450–6 (1993).

9. Passwater, R. A., "Heart disease and vitamin E study," *Prevention* 28(1):63–71 (1976).

10. Gey, K. Fred, Puska, Pekka, et al., "Inverse correlation between plasma vitamin E and mortality from ischemic heart disease in cross-cultural epidemiology," *Amer. J. Clin. Nutr.* 53:326S–334S (Jan. 1991).

11. Esterbauer, Hermann, et al., "The role of vitamin E and carotenoids in preventing oxidation of low-density lipoproteins," *Vitamin E: Biochemistry and Health Implications* (Diplock, A., et al. eds.). Ann. N. Y. Academy of Science 254–67 (1989).

12. Passwater, R. A. *The New Supernutrition.* Pocket Books, New York (1991).

13. Steinbrecher, U. P., Parthasarathy, S., et al., "Modification of low-density lipoprotein by endothelial cells involves lipid peroxidation and degradation of low-density lipoprotein phospholipids." Proc. Natl. Acad. Sci. 81:3883–7 (1984).

14. Gendre, Philippe M. J., Laparra, J. and Barraud, E., "Effet protecteur des oligomeres procyanidoliques sur le lathyrisme experimental chez le rat," *Annales Pharmaceutiques Francaises* 43(1):61–71 (1985).

15. Markle, Ronald A. and Hollis, Theodore M., "Variations in rabbit aortic endothelial and medial histamine synthesis in pre- and early atherosclerosis," Proc. Soc. Exper. Biol. Med. 155:365–8 (1977).

16. Hollis, Theodore M., and Furniss, John V., "Relationship between aortic histamine formation and aortic albumin permeability in atherosclerosis." Proc. Soc. Exper. Biol. Med. 165:271–4 (1980).

17. DeForrest, Jack M. and Hollis, Theodore M., "Shear stress and aortic histamine synthesis," *Amer. J. Physiol.* 234(6):H701–5 (1978).

18. Markle, Ronald A. and Hollis, Theodore M., "Rabbit aortic endothelial and medial histamine synthesis following short-term cholesterol feeding," *Exp. Mol. Path.* 23:417–25 (1975).

11

Dietary Antioxidants Versus Cancer

THE authors have extensive laboratory experience researching the roles of antioxidant nutrients in preventing cancer. Passwater has published on this subject since 1972, and his book, *Cancer Prevention and Nutritional Therapies,* originally published in 1978, was updated in 1993.[1,2] Passwater has concentrated primarily on the roles of the antioxidants vitamins A, C, and E, plus the trace mineral selenium and their mechanisms of protection. Kandaswami and his colleague Middleton have investigated the roles of various flavonoids in the prevention of enzymatic activation of carcinogens since the mid-1980s. We will review the basic mechanisms involved, and then turn our attention specifically to Pycnogenol. We will also discuss the antiviral roles of Pycnogenol and other flavonoids. This has implications for AIDS, post-polio syndrome and even the common cold.

Environmental chemicals, substances that are foreign to the body or *xenobiotics* (including those found in cigarette smoke and in food), have been linked to the causation of a majority of human cancers. Such cancer-causing chemicals (*carcinogens*) are believed to induce cancer by a two-stage process, namely initiation and promotion.

These chemical substances are thought to be activated to potentially noxious intermediate forms by certain enzymes which catalyze the oxidation of these chemicals. The intermediate forms bind firmly and irreversibly to DNA, the genetic material of a target cell, leading to certain changes in DNA. These mutations may be passed on to other cells, when the original cell divides. This sets off the process of initiation. Once cancer is initiated, it can be promoted by a number of factors, such as: other potentially toxic chemicals, fats, reactive oxygen species (ROS) including free radicals, and others.

In addition to the above enzyme-mediated processes, free radicals and oxidants have also been invoked in the initiation of cancer. Radicals are produced by exposure to environmental pollutants, radiation, drugs and alcohol, and by the body's own metabolism.

You may recall how free radicals can produce detrimental effects by causing damage to components such as DNA. We are equipped with a wide range of antioxidant defense systems, including the contribution of dietary antioxidants (both vitamin and nonvitamin antioxidant nutrients) in order to defend against ROS. Experimental studies show that dietary antioxidants such as vitamins C and E can protect animals against the induction of cancer. The role of ROS in the initiation and/or promotion of cancer has been inferred from such studies.

A huge volume of studies that examined the relationship between fruit and vegetable intake and cancers of several organs showed a significant protective effect of fruit and vegetable consumption.[3] Diets high in fruits and vegetables thus seem to provide the consumer with a variety of compounds possessing cancer-preventing effects. These nutrients include vitamins C and E as well as beta-carotene, each of which possesses antioxidant activity. In addition, diets rich in fruits and vegetables contain a multitude of flavonoids known as polyphenolic antioxidants with accompanying vitamin C-sparing activity. The average flavonoid intake from the diet appears to be far greater than that of vitamin E and beta-carotene. It is quite obvious that the cancer-protective effect of fruits and vegetables may not simply be due to the effect of vitamin C or beta-carotene, to give examples, as flavonoids abound in these foods. The protective effect is due to *all* these dietary substances. The body does not appear to use antioxidants individually. Instead, it seems to utilize them together as a defensive team.

Radical reactions have been implicated in inflammatory and immune responses. Disorders in the immune system can result in the secondary production of free radicals. In studies with mammalian cells, a wide variety of flavonoids has been shown to critically influence the functions of inflammatory and immune cells. Modulation of their function by flavonoids in disease states could afford protection against cancer.

Dietary administration of certain flavonoids like quercetin has been reported to protect experimental animals against mammary cancer and colon cancer induced by carcinogenic chemicals.[4,5] Application of quercetin and related flavonoids through the skin resulted in a lower incidence of skin cancer induced by carcinogenic chemicals commonly found in cigarette smoke.[6] You may recall how enzymes may be involved in converting cancer-causing chemicals to active forms in the cells which can initiate cancer. Flavonoids can interfere with the activity of these enzymes thus providing an ameliorative effect.[7] Certain flavonoids also abolish tumor promotion mediated by tumor promoters.[8] In these cases the flavonoids' effect could be due to its influence on key enzymes as well as interference with free-radical production caused by the promoters.

In addition to their cancer-preventing effect, flavonoids can also be useful in the treatment of fully progressed cancers.[9–11] Several studies showed that dietary administration of certain flavonoids significantly halted the growth of cancers in laboratory animals.[12] In these studies, cells from human tumors were allowed to grow in the animals and the effect of administration of the flavonoid on the growth of the cancer cells was evaluated. Certain flavonoids also were effective in stopping the spread of tumors (metastasis) in animals.

A variety of flavonoids were also shown to significantly arrest the growth of cancer cells in the laboratory.[12] In these studies, a variety of tumor cells, ranging from leukemia to prostate cancer cells, were grown in plastic dishes in the laboratory under controlled conditions, and the effect of treatment of the cells with different flavonoid compounds was assessed. These studies also reinforce the ability of flavonoids to interfere with the growth of cancers and their potential utility in cancer therapy.

Studies conducted in the laboratory of Dr. Kandaswami indicate that certain flavonoids, orally administered to rats, can induce hepatic enzymes that are involved in the metabolic transformation of certain carcinogens[7] Furthermore, liver preparations prepared from animals that were fed food flavonoids showed a reduced capacity to convert chemical carcinogens to their active forms. In other studies, we implanted tumor cells derived from human pharynx in the body cavity (peritoneum) of rats and evaluated the effect of the flavonoid quercetin on the growth of these cancer cells. Quercetin halted the growth of the tumor cells in a dose-dependent manner.[10]

We evaluated the efficacy of various food flavonoids in inhibiting the growth of cancer cells in a culture in the laboratory, as described above. Different classes of flavonoids significantly arrested the growth and survival of cells from several human cancers including: cancer of the pharynx, breast cancer, colon cancer, leukemia, brain cancer (gliosarcoma), and others.[7,13-16]

It is known that tumor cells can develop resistance to cancer drugs, this is called multidrug resistance. We found that luteolin, a food flavonoid, interfered with the growth of drug-resistant cultured cells of human breast cancer in the laboratory.

Pycnogenol is a powerful antioxidant radical scavenger and is a prime candidate for further studies in cancer prevention and therapy. This complex contains proanthocyanidins formed from catechin and epicatechin units. Certain catechin derivatives have recently been shown to have potent anticancer effects in experimental animals.[17-18]

Dr. David White of the University of Nottingham reported at a 1990 seminar on Pycnogenol in Bourdeaux, France that Pycnogenol inhibits the enzyme *monooxygenase*, thereby preventing the formation of the highly carcinogenic diole epoxide of benzo[a]pyrene, a major carcinogen of cigarette smoke. At the same meeting, Dr. Stewart Brown of the University of Nottingham reported that Pycnogenol's radical-scavenging ability slows cancer mutagenesis. Pycnogenol has also been shown to inhibit tumor promotion in skin.

Thus, one should consider the benefits of a diet rich in fruits and vegetables, plus the additional protection from the symphony of powerful flavonoids found in Pycnogenol.

For the Health Professional

We have conducted many studies of antioxidant nutrients through the years: Passwater on the role of various nutritional antioxidants in preventing the initiation of cancer, and Kandaswami and his colleague Middleton on the role of flavonoids in preventing the enzymatic activation of carcinogens. Research conducted by Kandaswami and Middleton indicated that dietary administration of certain citrus flavonoids (tangeretin and nobiletin) to rats resulted in the induction of enzymes in the liver mediating the biotransformation of benzo[a]pyrene.[7,19] Benzo[a]pyrene is a representative example of a class of chemical carcinogens known as polycyclic aromatic hydrocarbons. These compounds are ubiquitous environmental pollutants. They are present in cigarette smoke and in grilled meat. They are potent cancer-causing agents in animals.

Flavonoid-mediated induction of liver enzymes as observed above, could result in the increased detoxification of benzo[a]pyrene. Liver microsomes (membrane preparations rich in enzymes) prepared from rats that received oral supplementation of the flavonoids, tangeretin or nobiletin, were less effective in converting benzo[a]pyrene to active intermediates that bind DNA, when compared to liver microsomes from rats that did not receive any oral administration of the flavonoid.

The formation of the DNA-binding intermediate compounds from the parent carcinogen (e.g. benzo[a]pyrene) is considered to be a critical event in cancer induction process. Dietary administration of quercetin to rats was also observed to stimulate the induction of certain liver enzymes which participate in the detoxification of the carcinogen. These observations suggest some modes of action by which flavonoids can exert cancer protection.

In view of the ability of flavonoids to influence carcinogen-metabolizing enzyme activities, they can conceivably play a cardinal role in nutrition from the point of view of dietary modulation of cancer induction. Since human exposure to dietary flavonoids is essentially universal (assuming consumption of copious amounts of fruits and vegetables), they can play a pivotal role in affecting the induction and promotion of cancer.

We evaluated the effect of the flavonoid quercetin on the growth of cancer cells of human pharynx (squamous cell carcinoma) in rats.[11] Growth chambers were implanted subcutaneously in immunologically competent rats treated with quercetin. The growth of cancer cells was found to be significantly impaired by quercetin. A similar effect was found on the growth of cancer cells (human squamous cell carcinoma) from the tongue. We also found that several flavonoids impaired the growth and survival of human cancer cells grown in cultures in the laboratory. Quercetin and fisetin inhibited the proliferation of squamous cell carcinoma cells. Tangeretin and nobiletin are two citrus flavonoids. All their phenolic groups are substituted by methyl groups. These flavonoids (methoxylated flavonoids) greatly reduced the growth and survival of the above cancer cells. Interestingly, the proliferation of normal human lung cells (fibroblast-like cells) was not affected by quercetin or other flavonoids at concentrations at which they impaired the growth of cancer cells. In addition, the cancer cell growth-inhibitory action of the flavonoids, fisetin and quercetin, was considerably enhanced by vitamin C. The effect of the vitamin may be due to its ability to protect the flavonoids against degradation. It appears that flavonoids and vitamin C protect each other. This interaction could be important in fulfilling the optimal health-protective effects of both the flavonoids and vitamin C. The above studies indicate that flavonoids, which are common dietary constituents, can play an effective role in cancer prevention/amelioration.

Our studies showed that the flavonoids *luteolin* can inhibit the proliferation of multi-drug-resistant human breast cancer cells.[16] Another interesting observation concerns the effect of flavonoids on certain enzymes involved in the growth of cancer cells. Our recent studies showed that flavonoids such as luteolin and quercetin abolished the activity of protein tyrosine kinases in certain cancer cells in culture, such as HeLa cells.[20] These enzymes are products of oncogenes which are involved in malignant growth. The expression of these enzymes is elevated or modified in tumor cells. These enzymes mediate the signal for increased cell growth. Impairment of the activity of these enzymes by flavonoids indicates that they can effectively control the progression of malignancy.

Other potential cancer-related effects of flavonoids include causing the differentiation of malignant cells to normal cells, and the inhibition of the generation of new capillaries (*angiogenesis*). Solid tumor growth and metastasis are associated with extensive generation of new capillaries. Flavonoids have been shown to inhibit this process.

The control of neoplasia by antiproliferative and cancer cell differentiating agents appears to be an exciting prospect. To date, only vitamin A and retinoid derivatives have shown promise in clinical trials as agents which might reverse early steps in malignant growth. The toxicity of these compounds has limited their widespread utility. The flavonoids appear to be promising in this regard.

REFERENCES

1. Passwater, R. A., "Cancer: New directions," *Amer. Lab.* 5(6): 10–22 (1973).

2. Passwater, R. A., *Cancer Prevention and Nutritional Therapies* Keats Publishing, Inc., New Canaan, Conn. (1993).

3. Block, G., Paterson, B. and Subar, A., *Nutr. Cancer* 18:1 (1992).

4. Verma, A. K., Johnson, J. A., et al., *Cancer Res.* 48:5754 (1988).

5. Deschner, E. E., Ruperto, J., et al., *Carcinogenesis* 12:1193 (1991).

6. Mukhtar, H., Das, M., et al., *Cancer Res.* 48:2361 (1988).

7. Middleton, E., Jr. and Kandaswami, C., *Adjuvant Nutrition in Cancer Treatment* (M. R. Williams and P. Quillin, eds.). Cancer Treatment Research Foundation, Arlington Heights, Illinois (1993).

8. Kato, R., Nakadate, T., et al., *Carcinogenesis* 4:1301 (1983).

9. Edwards, M., Raffauf, R. F., and Quesne, W. L., *J. Nat. Prod.* 42:85 (1979).

10. Molnar, J., Beladi, I., et al., *Neoplasma* 28:11 (1981).

11. Castillo, M. H., Perkins, E., et al., *Am. J. Surg.* 158:351 (1989).

12. Middleton, Jr., E. and Kandaswami, C., *The Flavonoids: Advances in Research Since 1986* (J. B. Harborne, ed.). Chapman & Hall, London, 619 (1993).

13. Kandaswami, C., Perkins, E., Soloniuk, D. S., et al., *Cancer Letters* 56:147 (1991).

14. Kandaswami, C., Perkins, E., Soloniuk, D. S., et al., *Anti-Cancer Drugs* 3:525 (1992).

15. Kandaswami, C., Perkins, E., et al., *Anti-Cancer Drugs* 4:91 (1993).

16. Kandaswami, C., Perkins, E., et al. (in preparation).

17. Wang, Z. Y., Huang, M. T., et al., *Cancer Res.* 52:6657 (1992).

18. Tangiguchi, S., and Fujiki, H., et al., *Cancer Letters* 65:51 (1992).

19. Kandaswami, C. and Middleton, Jr., E. (in preparation).

20. Lee, M. T., Middleton, Jr., E., and Kandaswami, C. (in preparation).

12

Other Important Relationships

THERE are many other important ways in which Pycnogenol helps maintain optimal health. There is preliminary evidence that Pycnogenol improves mental function, protects against the effects of stress, reduces some of the side effects of diabetes, and may even help improve vision.

The strength of the evidence varies from laboratory studies to anecdotal, but since the mechanism believed to be involved has been proven in other studies, these relationships should be given serious consideration.

Brain Function

Pycnogenol is important to brain function, not only because it protects blood vessels, but also because some of its bioflavonoids readily cross the blood-brain barrier to directly protect brain cells. The blood-brain barrier protects the brain from many compounds that normally circulate in the blood. Brain cells need lots of oxygen. (It is amazing how much oxygen this organ consumes!) Blood supplies the brain with oxygen, but since brain cells are very sensitive to some compounds that circulate in blood—even though those compounds may not damage other cells in the body or may even be needed by other cells—the brain filters out as many nonessential compounds as it can. This is accomplished by the so-called blood-brain-barrier.

Protection of brain cells helps memory and reduces senility. There are indications that even sluggish memories are improved, perhaps due to better circulation and cell nourishment. German studies have shown that the bioflavonoids of *Ginkgo biloba* are important to brain function and several studies have indicated that the Ginkgo flavonoids significantly improve memory function.

Stress and Ulcers

Acute hemorrhagic ulcers of the esophagus, stomach and duodenum are common today. They can result in serious gastrointestinal bleeding and death. Although exciting new evidence suggests that many ulcers are the result of action of the bacterium *Helicobacter pylori* (also *campylobacter pylori*), histamine may still be involved in the pathogenesis of stress ulcer disease. As discussed in Chapter Three, Pycnogenol inhibits the enzyme *histidine decarboxylase*, and thus lowers histamine levels.

Because Pycnogenol prevents excessive histamine release, it has been shown to reduce stress ulcers in the stomach and intestine by 82 percent.[1] This has been confirmed by Dr. Duncan Bell of England's Ipswich Hospital and reported at the 1990 International Symposium on Pycnogenol.[2] Dr. Bell, a gastroenterologist, reported on the antistress action of Pycnogenol and how it prevents ulcer formation.

Diabetes

Diabetics in particular are prone to vascular fragility. Pycnogenol reduces this fragileness. Pycnogenol's protective effect on capillaries extends even to the delicate capillaries of the eyes. The damage to the retina caused by the microbleeding of the eye capillaries due to diabetes is one of the more common causes of blindness in adults.

In fact, Pycnogenol has been licenced in France for years for treating diabetic retinopathy. This usage was first based on clinical studies of 40 patients by Dr. G. Maynard and colleagues. The patients were given 80 to 120 milligrams of Pycnogenol daily for a week, and then maintained on 40 to 80 milligrams daily for 1.5 to 4 months.

The microbleeding of the capillaries decreased remarkably in 90 percent of the patients and their eyesight improved noticeably.

Professor Saracco of the Clinic for Ophthalmology in Marseille studied 60 patients and confirmed that Pycnogenol improved diabetic retinopathy and hypertensive retinopathy, as well as reduced loosening of the retina itself.

Other French physicians have concluded that Pycnogenol is the first choice in the treatment of diabetic retinopathy.

A German medical researcher, Professor H. C. W. Leydhecker, found that Pycnogenol compares favorably with any other current treatments for diabetic retinopathy.[3] Dr. Leydhecker, Director of the University Eye Clinic in Wurzburg at the time, compared the effectiveness of Pycnogenol with the drug Dexium (calcium dobesilate). Dexium is routinely used to suppress the progress of diabetic retinopathy. There were 16 patients in each group, but it was impractical to assign a placebo group because the patients were referred to the study from private practice. Seven university professors evaluated the photographs of the patients' retinas before and after treatment, without being aware of which patients were taking which compound. After six months of treatment, both compounds were found to be indeed effective and equally so.

Problems with Eyesight

In the study just described, many patients also experienced improved visual acuity. Similarly, a small-scale clinical research project designed to study diabetic retinopathy was conducted by Dr. Emilio Balestrazzi of the University of Aquila in Italy. He concluded:

"The overall clinical judgement on pycnogenol, compared with the control groups treated with placebo, and taking account of all the clinical and instrumental tests and the absence of side effects, is to be considered beneficial, in as much as all patients benefited to a varying degree from the treatment. In fact, the effects on the resistance and the peripheral capillary permeability of the vessels have shown themselves to be positive in improving the functioning of the retina.''

The herb bilberry (*Vaccinum myrtillus*), has been shown to improve eyesight. During World War II, pilots relied on bilberry for improved vision. The flavonoids in bilberry were the active compounds.

Interestingly, we have ancedotal reports from various individuals that their diabetes has been brought under better control while using Pycnogenol. As an example, a pilot was finally able to pass his medical exam for a commercial license after years and years of trying. The number of reports suggests that at least a small study to test this premise would be in order.

Arthritis

Several anecdotal reports note that arthritics feel improvement *overnight* with a bedtime dose of 120–150 milligrams of Pycnogenol. Since both osteoarthritis and rheumatoid arthritis are inflammatory diseases, Pycnogenol may help by quenching some of the free radicals that are involved in the inflammatory process.

The ability of Pycnogenol to improve joint flexibility and repair the collagen in connective tissue should also be of interest to arthritics. Many bioflavonoids inhibit the enzymes (*elastases*) and prostaglandins that lead to inflammation, but Pycnogenol is particularly effective.[4]

Pycnogenol also inhibits histamine release, which further reduces inflammation. As mentioned in Chapter Six, histamine is one of the more important mediators in allergic and inflammatory reactions. At the 1990 International Symposium on Pycnogenol, Dr. David White of the University of Nottingham reported that Pycnogenol greatly reduces the formation of histamine, and thus reduces painful and crippling inflammation.

Pycnogenol inhibits the degranulation of mast cells. Mast cells are large cells with coarse granules that contain histamine. The connective tissue is well-supplied with mast cells. Mast cells are mediators of inflammation upon contact with antigens. When mast cells are degranulated, histamine is liberated from the stock inside the mast cell, the granula. Pycnogenol reduces the liberation of histamine and can thus reduce arthritic inflammation.

Antiviral Effects of Flavonoids

Naturally occurring flavonoids with antiviral activity have been recognized since the 1940s.[5] Quercetin, morin, rutin, taxifolin (found in Pycnogenol and other sources, also called dihydroquercetin), dihydrofisetin, leucocyanidin (found in Pycnogenol and other sources), pelargonidin chloride, apigenin, catechin (found in Pycnogenol and other sources), hesperitin and naringin have been reported to possess antiviral activity against some of 11 types of viruses.[5] The antiviral activity appears to be associated with nonglycosidic compounds.

In Belgium, investigations on the constituents responsible for pronounced antiviral activity found in extracts of *Euphorbia grantii* stems have provided four flavonoids that exhibit significant activities against picornaviruses and vesicular stomatitis virus.[6] All of the active antiviral compounds were derivatives of quercetin. Mice were protected from viremia and lethal infection from coxsackie B4 virus by these compounds when administered at a dose of 20 mg/kg for a period of nine days.

Naturally occurring flavonoids were shown to inhibit rhino- and poliomyelitis viruses.[7] Several flavonoids inhibited human herpes simplex virus type 1 (HSV-1) and other herpes viruses.[8] Quercetin, catechin (found in Pycnogenol and other sources) and other flavonoids reduced the infectivity and replication of HSV-1, poliovirus type 1, parainfluenza virus type e and respiratory syncytial virus.[9] Recently reported pharmacological effects of flavonoids and structurally related plant polyphenols could have implications in AIDS therapy. The flavonoid *baicalein* (5,6,7-trihydroxyflavone) isolated from the medicinal plant *Scutellaria baicalensis* inhibited a human immunodeficiency virus (HIV) infection of cells and replication of the virus in studies employing cell culture in the laboratory.[10] This flavone was found to be a potent and highly specific inhibitor of HIV reverse transcriptase.[11] Baicalein also inhibited the replication of human T-cell leukemia virus (HTLV-1) in a concentration-dependent manner.[12] Baicalein is known to be a powerful antioxidant. The impairment of the infectivity and replication of HIV and other viruses by this naturally occurring, nontoxic flavonoid is a clear indication of the potential role of flavonoids in disease prevention.

The Future

As we stated in the beginning of this book, the nutritional roles of flavonoids have long been neglected, but they are certain to become the nutritional stars of the twenty-first century. There are many, many flavonoids to study, but you can be sure that Pycnogenol will receive serious and increasing scientific interest in the coming years. As more and more physicians and health care providers recommend Pycnogenol as a food supplement, we will receive many more fascinating reports that can be investigated clinically.

REFERENCES

1. Reimann, H. J.; Lorenz, W.; Fischer, M.; Frolich, R.; Meyer, H. J. and Schmal, A. Histamine and acute hemorrhagic lesions in rat gastric mucosa: Prevention of stress ulcer by catechin. *Agents Actions* 7(1):6972 (1977).

2. Bell, Duncan, International Symposium on Pycnogenol. Bordeaux, France (Oct. 1990).

3. Leydhecker, H. C. W., Scientific report on the effectivity and tolerance of Pycnogenol in treating diabetic retinopathy based on clinical comparative test. University Eye Clinic, Wurzburg, Germany.

4. Tixier, J. M., Godeau, G., et al., Evidence by in vivo and in

vitro studies that binding of Pycnogenols to elastin affects its rate of degradation by elastases. *Biochem. Pharmacol.* 33(24):3933–9 (1984).

5. Selway, J. W. T., *Plant Flavonoids in Biology and Medicine* (V. Cody, E. Middleton, and J. B. Harborne, eds.). Alan R. Liss, Inc., New York, 521 (1986).

6. Van Hoof, L., Vanden, Berghe, D. A., Hatfield, G. M. and Vlietinck, A. J.: *Planta Medica* 50:513 (1984).

7. DeMeyer, N., Haemers, A., et al., *J. Med. Chem.* 34:736 (1991).

8. Mucsi, I. and Pragai, B. M., *Experientia* 41:6 (1985).

9. Kaul, T. N., Middleton, Jr., E. and Ogra, P. L., *J. Med. Virol.* 15:71 (1985).

10. Li, B. Q., Yan, Y. D., et al., *Cell Mol. Biol. Res.* 39:119 (1993).

11. Ono, K., Nakane, H., et al., *Biochem. Biophys. Res. Commun.* 160:982 (1989).

12. Baylor, N. W., Fu, T., et al., *J. Infect. Dis.* 165:433 (1992).

13

Pycnogenol's Proven Safety

PYCNOGENOL has not only withstood the test of time, it was extensively tested before it was made available as a food supplement. Pycnogenol was first made available in Europe as an over-the-counter drug because the European health system was more conducive to this approach. As a result, Pycnogenol has been consumed in Europe under medical supervision for decades and in the United States for many years with no reports of adverse effects. Millions of Pycnogenol capsules and tablets are taken every day.

Pycnogenol has been tested and tested again according to conventional safety standards at several prestigious centers, including: the Pasteur Institute in Lyon, France, and the Cytotest Cell Research (CCR) in Darmstadt, Germany.[1,2] Researchers at these world-renowned centers concluded that Pycnogenol is nontoxic, nonteratogenic, nonmutagenic, noncarcinogenic and nonantigenic.[3-6]

Passwater traveled to Germany and Finland to investigate the safety of Pycnogenol. In Germany, the safety of Pycnogenol was discussed with Peter Rohdewald, Ph.D. Dr. Rohdewald is a professor and the former commissarial director of the Institute for Pharmaceutical Chemistry at the University of Muenster. He is also the co-author of two textbooks on pharmaceutical analytical investigations, and has published dozens of scientific articles on pharmacokinetics, bioavailability and the efficacy of pharmaceuticals. Here is an excerpt from that lengthy and fascinating interview:

QUESTION: How long has Pycnogenol been studied and how long have you been studying it?

ROHDEWALD: Pycnogenol has been studied since 1953, and I have been studying it since 1982.

QUESTION: As a pharmacist, you also have extensive training in toxicology. I have read several independent toxicological studies on Pycnogenol in which you served as the study monitor. What can you tell us about the safety of Pycnogenol?

ROHDEWALD: Yes, as a pharmacist, I am involved with toxicity studies. The composition of Pycnogenol tells us a lot about its safety. We have completely identified and characterized more than 85 percent of the ingredients in Pycnogenol and all of these substances but taxifolin are found in other plants that have been used in human nutrition over the centuries. As you know, the main constituents are natural antioxidants called proanthocyanidins which are also contained in foods such as sorghum, avocado, strawberries, bananas, and others.

There are small quantities of other nutrients in the extract such as caffeic acid, cinnamic acid, fumaric acid, gallic acid, vanillic acid, ferulic acid and related substances. You can tell from the names of these nutrients that they are found in other plants. Caffeic acid and ferulic acid are found in parsley and spinach. Caffeic acid is also found in onions, ferulic acid is also found in rhubarb and grapes, fumaric acid in chives and beetroot, and gallic acid in aubergine (eggplant) and radish. Also present are vanillic acid and protocatechuic acid which are proven antioxidants and anti-inflammatory substances.

Caffeic acid helps protect the liver against toxic substances and both caffeic acid and ferulic acid stimulate transport of bile from the liver cells to the gall bladder. Both are excellent free-radical scavengers and they prevent the formation of *nitroso* compounds of amino acids. Nitroso compounds are carcinogens which can be produced within the gastrointestinal tract.

Even though these nutrients are available in other vegetables, fruits, spices and beverages, Pycnogenol has the advantage of providing these valuable nutrients in a concentrated form. However, because there is a greater potency due to this concentration, it is extremely important the extract be tested for adverse effects. Just because it is a natural plant extract, doesn't mean that a concentration of these natural compounds could not have adverse effects. Therefore intensive investigations using laboratory mice, rats, guinea pigs, dogs and even minipigs have been performed to see if Pycnogenol does any harm. There have also been studies to determine if Pycnogenol has any mutagenic, carcinogenic or adverse effects in pregnant animals. The outcome of these many studies is that Pycnogenol has been shown by accepted toxicological protocols to not be mutagenic, carcinogenic, teratogenic or toxic. It is safe, as could be expected from its composition.

The Ames test for mutagenicity was carried out in the Pasteur Institute in Lyon, France in 1971. The micronucleus assay in mouse bone marrow cells and chromosome aberration assay in human lymphocytes were performed by Dr. Albrecht Heidemann at Cytotest Cell Research GmbH (CCR) in Darmstadt, Germany in 1989 and they were also negative. Pycnogenol is not mutagenic or carcinogenic.

Tests for teratogenesis (birth defects) has been carried out on mice and rabbits by Professor G. C. Pantaleoni at the University of Aquila in Italy and on mice, rabbits and rats at the Institute for Bioresearch in Hanover, Germany during 1967 to 1971, and by Dr. J. Laparra of the University of Bordeaux, France in 1975. Pycnogenol is not embryotoxic or teratogenic. It will not adversely influence perinatal toxicity or fertility.

Acute and chronic toxicities have been tested in several species including mice, rats, guinea pig and dog at both the University of Aquila and the Institute for Bioresearch. Pycnogenol is normally consumed in milligram amounts. Chronic toxicity tests with dogs indicate that adverse effects would not be produced in man until 35,000 milligrams of Pycnogenol were taken daily for more than six months. Acute toxicity tests in dogs indicates that human acute toxicity could occur at 336 grams (336,000 milligrams) in a typical 155-pound male. Pycnogenol has a very low acute toxicity. Experimenters could not cause death by an intrinsic toxicity, but only as a result of osmotic effects due to the extremely large quantities that had to be administered to cause such a result. Pycnogenol is safe from a pharmacological point of view.

In Finland, the question of Pycnogenol safety was discussed with Dr. Antti Holevi Arstila, M.D., a cell biologist, toxicologist, pathologist and antioxidant expert. He is the Chairman of the Department of Cell Biology at the University of Jyvaeskylae in Jyvaeskylae, Finland. Professor Arstila has authored 15 scientific and medical textbooks, in addition to six books for laymen on health and disease. He has also contributed to more than 200 scientific publications, congress abstracts and textbooks on subjects that include electron microscopy, neuroscience, cell injury, lipid peroxidation, free radicals and antioxidants.

QUESTION: You have written books on toxicology. What can you tell us about the safety of Pycnogenol?

ARSTILA: Pycnogenol was well-tested before it was introduced in Europe, and it has been well-tested throughout the years to keep up with the increased sophistication of toxicological tests. As an example, Pycnogenol has been subjected to tests for mutagenicity, carcinogenicity, teratogenic [birth defects] and acute and gross toxicities in several species of animals. Many clinical studies have been made and no adverse effects have been reported. Pycnogenol has received extensive toxicity testing in comparison to food supplements such as vitamins, because of its widespread use by physicians in Europe.

The manufacturer of Pycnogenol, Horphag Research Ltd., continually monitors its safety with routine toxicological tests. While the key rule of toxicology is that everything—including oxygen and water—becomes toxic at a high enough dose, Pycnogenol is safe as a daily food supplement when used as recommended.

REFERENCES

1. Yu, C. L. and Swaminathan, B., "Mutagenicity of proanthocyanidins." *Food Chem. Toxicol.* 25(2):135–9 (1987).

2. Pantaleoni, G. C., Quaglino, D., University of Aquila Pharmaco-Toxicologica Report.

3. Laparra, J., et al., *Acta Therapeutica* 4:233 (1978).

4. *Ibid.* #1

5. Volkner, Wolfgang and Muller, Ewald, Micronucleus assay in bone marrow cells of the mouse with Pycnogenol. Cytotest Cell Research GmbH & Co., projects 143010 & 143021 (Feb. 1989).

6. Acute and chronic toxicity tests. International Bio-Research, Inc., Hanover, Germany.

14

The Making of Pycnogenol
and Pycnogenol Supplements

BEFORE you read about Pycnogenol supplements, remember: Pycnogenol is not a *single* nutrient, but a *mixture* prepared under a commercial process. Pycnogenol is a blend of monomers, dimers, oligomers and organic acids, and this blend must be consistent from one production lot to another. We have determined that indeed this is the case according to our study of production lots from 1991 through 1993. We assume that through the decades manufacturing plants and methods may have improved, but that the product has been held constant. However, we have no samples produced prior to 1991 for testing.

Secondly, we have strived to assure to the best of our ability, that it is this precise blend that has been used in the tests described in this book. This blend has been studied and manufactured for decades and is the product used in the studies presented in this book. We are limiting our discussion to the topic of Pycnogenol as much as possible to avoid confusion between various bioflavonoids which do differ markedly in their biochemical actions.

Thirdly, other preparations must be proven in their own clinical studies. One cannot assume that a "similar" preparation will be equivalent, because Nature gives each plant a unique mix of bioflavonoids. In addition, because of extraction differences, the resultant blend will not be identical. As mentioned in Chapter Four, Dr. Zhao Guochang summarizes this best in his doctoral dissertation done at the University of Jyvaeskylae in Finland:

"Natural extracts contain different complex ingredients. Different extraction methods may obtain different ingredients. Extracts from different sources may contain different components. Even within the same group of flavonoids, molecular structure varies among extracts from different natural sources."

The molecular structures that represent the proanthocyanidins of Pycnogenol are unique and have proven benefits.

Pycnogenol has been licensed to Horphag Research Ltd, a company that has been sponsoring Pycnogenol research for decades. In France, Dr. Passwater learned more about the production of Pycnogenol from Horphag Research's CEO, chemist Charles Haimoff.

In the 1950s Horphag Research evaluated several plant sources for the extraction of proanthocyanidins, but the maritime pines found growing in the area of Bordeaux, France south to the Spanish border were chosen for several reasons in addition to the historic source dating back to before the sixteenth century. This area has no commercial farming and no industrial centers. This virtually synthetic-chemical-free environment is bathed in the fresh air of the Atlantic. The maritime pine being a tree grown on nutrient-rich virgin ground, has not been subjected to pesticides or fertilizers which besides possibly contaminating the product, can over decades of use, play havoc with the genetic make-up of plants. In addition, the bark of the maritime pine is practically free of oxidants, metals and alkaline substances that could also be extracted with the proanthocyanidins. This means that the product can be all antioxidant and no oxidant, which is better for the consumer and yields a more stable product having longer shelf life (ten years or more).

Horphag Research testing ensures that Pycnogenol is produced under rigorous control so that the effects of climate or the growing season do not alter the extracted blends of flavonoids. One ton of maritime pine bark will yield about 2.5 kilograms of Pycnogenol depending on the season. The Pycnogenol compounds are extracted with warm water and pressure and then precipitated from the water by adding an organic salt to the water. The exclusive extraction process and the resultant precipitation does not damage the chemical structures of any of the components of Pycnogenol. Since they are extracted by water only, the compounds of Pycnogenol are all water-soluble. The manufacturing plant performing the Pycnogenol production makes no other products which could cross-contaminate the Pycnogenol.

Over decades of clinical testing and use, the maritime pine has turned out to be a fortunate source indeed. The blend of catechins, dimers, oligomers and organic acids has been particularly effective. Remember that each plant specie produces its own array of flavonoids. The oligomers of the maritime pine are unique and account for the power and versatility of Pycnogenol.

More than 85 percent of the compounds in Pycnogenol have been characterized. Pycnogenol contains not only proanthocyanidins, but also contains other water-soluble nutrients. These nutrients are building blocks for the bio-synthesis of proanthocyanidins in the living plant and are extracted together with the proanthocyanidins from the pine bark. Catechin, epicatechin and taxifolin are called monomers of proanthocyanidins (although they do not produce a red color on hydrolysis).

Pycnogenol also contains small amounts of other substances called organic acids including caffeic acid, cinnamic acid, fumaric acid, gallic acid, vanillic acid, ferulic acid and related substances. These "minor" organic acids make a significant and positive contribution to the beneficial effects of Pycnogenol. About one-third of Pycnogenol consists of monomers and organic acids, one-third is dimers and trimers, and the remaining third consists of tetramers and higher oligomers.

Just as vitamin C or vitamin E are commodities, so it is with Pycnogenol—although Pycnogenol is patented. It is a registered trademark of Horphag Research Ltd. which allows the product to be used by various companies in the manufacture of food supplements. Just as you can buy vitamin C or E in many formulations from many companies, you can purchase Pycnogenol from many companies in several formulations.

Pycnogenol is usually sold by itself in various strengths, but it is also increasingly being used in antioxidant formulations and multiple vitamin formulations. It is available as a pure material, or mixed with fillers in capsules, or blended with binders (such as dicalcium phosphate) and pressed as tablets. Dicalcium phosphate is often chosen as a filler because it is a source of calcium and has a proven safety record with many years of usage in the health food and pharmaceutical industries.

We realize that we haven't been able to answer all of your questions about Pycnogenol in this book. There is still more research to do. Good health!